FOREWORD BY MIKE BICKLE

# INVITATION TO ENCOUNTER

A JOURNEY IN DREAMS

JULIE MEYER

*Invitation to Encounter*
By Julie Meyer

Published by Forerunner Books
International House of Prayer–Kansas City
3535 East Red Bridge Road
Kansas City, Missouri 64137
(816) 763-0200 Ext. 2675
*forerunnerbooks@ihop.org*
*www.IHOP.org*

ISBN: 978-0-9798807-6-6

Unless otherwise noted, all Scripture quotations are from the *New
King James Version* of the Bible. Copyright © 1979, 1980, 1982 by
Thomas Nelson, Inc., publishers.

Scripture quotations marked KJV are from the *King James Version* of
the Bible.

Scripture quotations marked NAS are from the *New American Stan-
dard Bible.* Copyright © 1960, 1962, 1963, 1968, 1971, 1972, 1973,
1975, 1977 by the Lockman Foundation.

Cover design by Ben Hoeppner
Interior design by Dale Jimmo
Edited by Josh Farmer and Jennifer Sansom

Printed in the United States of America

# Table of Contents

# Endorsements

If you think that reading a series of someone else's dreams would be boring, then you have yet to give this book a fair chance. You will find it insightful, heartwarming, and intriguing. Read this book prayerfully and you'll gain a portal into some of the mysteries of God's heart, how He feels about you, and what He has in store for our planet.

—Bob Sorge, Author, Founder of Oasis House Ministries

Nothing is more enjoyable than new discoveries of the knowledge of God. As Julie shares her dreams, we all get to see His ancient attributes in a new light. Julie Meyer is a gifted writer and *Invitation to Encounter* is a beautiful book.

—Wesley and Stacey Campbell, Authors, Founders of Be A Hero

Julie Meyer is one of my heroes of the faith. She is small in stature, yet some of the most profound, powerful prophetic discourses I have ever heard flow from her in full volume. She has gleaned valuable Kingdom nuggets and insights into God's mysteries through living a lifestyle of focused worship and intercession. This book reveals some of those treasures. I want to absorb it all. You will too.

    —Patricia King, Author, Founder of Extreme Prophetic

Julie Meyer is a passionate lover of Jesus. The heights of prophetic insight she reaches are matched by the depth of her humility, integrity, and commitment to the Word of God. She can be trusted. Her insights will fuel the spiritual pilgrim on the journey to Zion.

    —Robert Stearns, Author, Executive Director of Eagles'
      Wings

In this compilation of dreams, Julie Meyer reveals the creative nature of God, one aspect of His identity. Julie is one of those people whose particular gift is to creatively unveil the expressive nature of God through music, dreams and visions, and through the revelation of His glory on Earth. Because I love that aspect of God's identity, I love Julie. She makes me dance; she makes me wonder; she makes me cry; she helps me tap into that childlike spirit God has given to me as well as to all of us. I love what she wrote in this book. When you read this book, you will enter the door to peek at Heaven coming to Earth.

    —Barbara Yoder, Author, Senior Pastor and Lead Apostle
      of Shekinah Christian Church

It's a delight for me to recommend this volume of prophetic dreams to you. My wife Marie and I have been tremendously encouraged by what the Lord has spoken through Julie over the years, and we have been inspired to deeper intercession and holiness as a result. Julie's visions of Heaven were a source of great comfort and strength for my family during a time of personal tragedy. May the Holy Spirit use these revelations to inspire you to a deeper life of intercession and faith as you walk out the journey the Lord has prepared for you.

—Gary Wiens, Author, President of Burning Heart
    Ministries

Julie Meyer is a prophetic singer who carries the glory and the presence of God as an abandoned worshipper. Raging hunger drove her to contend for deeper realms of God's presence, and over time, dreams and visions began to break into her life. Julie shares these compelling encounters with such transparency and passion that it arrests the soul of even the most diligent seeker. As you read these accounts, your heart will be challenged and tenderized as Julie takes you on journeys that go deep into the heart of Jesus. You'll begin to see things from His perspective and receive revelation that changes how you see Jesus and yourself. *Invitation to Encounter: A Journey In Dreams* will whet your appetite and help you realize that divine encounters are attainable. Let the journey of your heart begin!

—Jill Austin, Author, Founder/President of Master Potter
    Ministries

It is with great joy that we commend to you the writings and revelation that the Lord has given to His servant and our friend Julie Meyer. We know no one who moves in greater clarity and prayerful wisdom in their dreams than this chosen prophetic vessel. As you read the pages of this book, the spirit of prayer and revelation of the Holy Spirit will jump all over you!

—James W. and Michal Ann Goll, Authors, Cofounders of
    Encounters Network

From the first time I met Julie, I knew there was something special about this woman. Her abandoned devotion to the Lord and her deep intimacy with Him are evident, whether she is worshipping, speaking or just being herself. As you read this book, a compilation of her spiritual dreams, you will hear the heart of God, and hopefully you will be inspired to say with her, "God, I want more of You in my life." Be blessed as you read.

—Jane Hansen Hoyt, Author, President of Aglow
   International

I've known Julie Meyer personally for twenty-five years now. We sort of grew up in the prophetic side-by-side in Kansas City. I have nothing but the highest regard for her life in God and the newfound place of spiritual encounter I have watched Him bestow upon her. Julie's dreams and encounters are among the highest I have come across, and I love the way she is able to express the truths of Scripture in the midst of it all! You will be greatly impacted by this journey of hers as recorded in her encounters in God, all of which are biblically sound and steeped in what the Lord is saying to the Church today. He who has ears to hear, let him hear what the Spirit is saying to us through her profound journey. Receive the invitation and allow it to be a catalyst in your own walk with God.

—JoAnn McFatter, Recording Artist, Founder of Inside
   Eternity

We are presently living in a time of prophetic destiny and scriptural fulfillment. Never has the need been greater to be awakened to the Spirit's realm and to cultivate personal exchange and intimate fellowship with the Lord in order to be positioned for our individual destiny and cooperation with Heaven. Julie Meyer has beautifully captured this reality in her book, *Invitation to Encounter: A Journey in Dreams.* Her revelatory experiences and biblical insights will provide keys that unlock God's mysteries for an end-time army to arise in revelation and power. Although the insights are captivating, this book is more an invitation to find your place in God and walk with Him like Enoch did. *Invitation to Encounter* will be a fruitful addition to the library of every hungry heart.

    —Paul Keith Davis, Author, Founder of White Dove
      Ministries

*The Creation of Light*

# Dedication

I would like to dedicate this book to my Beloved Savior, Jesus Christ, who spoke to me in these joyful dreams and revealed to me His wonderful kindness and tender mercy. He also extended an invitation to me to "come and sit a while" with Him that has truly been a blessing to me.

To my dear husband, Walt: you are my best friend. Also, my sons Jesse, Joseph and Isaac, and our beautiful daughter-in-law Brittany, Isaac's bride. I love you all very much!

*Jesus at the House of Martha and Mary*

# Foreword

Julie Meyer and I have been friends since she was a college student. I first met her when she sang for the youth group of the church I was pastoring in St. Louis, Missouri. She was young and still growing in the prophetic, but her voice was anointed. I knew the Lord was going to do something special with her and use her to touch the nations.

Over the years, I have seen her mature spiritually and become more confident in her prophetic singing. She sings to God and from God, and has blessed many through her singing ministry. In the last few years, she has begun to cultivate her prophetic gifting in relation to the dreams she has received from the Lord. Many others would become puffed up with pride if they were given such dreams. Julie stewards her dreams and prays them faithfully, aware of the responsibilities the Lord has given her.

Julie's prophetic dreams are given in the context of her commitment to walk in humility in her relationship with Jesus. I have watched her go through seasons of promotion and demotion and come out unoffended. In each encounter she has had with the Lord, she seeks to die to herself and to grow in the knowledge of God. She has gone on a journey of prayer and humility. I value these prophetic dreams because they extend to us an invitation to go on that same journey of humility. The joy that Julie has found is available to you, because everyone can encounter the Lord. Everyone can pray, pursue intimacy and seek Him. His desire is for us to know Him and to be with Him where He is (John 17:24).

I pray that you will meet Jesus in a profound way as you read this book. God is looking for those who will hear what He is saying to the Church in this hour of history and will respond in prayer, asking for His will to be fulfilled and seeking His face. He is looking for friends who will humble themselves before Him in worship, who will find joy in the lowest places, and who are willing to go on this journey with Him. No matter what your circumstances, the invitation to encounter is open to all.

*Mike Bickle*
Director of the International House of Prayer
Kansas City, Missouri

# Introduction

BUT AS IT IS WRITTEN: "EYE HAS NOT SEEN, NOR EAR
HEARD, NOR HAVE ENTERED INTO THE HEART OF MAN
THE THINGS WHICH GOD HAS PREPARED FOR THOSE
WHO LOVE HIM." BUT GOD HAS REVEALED THEM TO
US THROUGH HIS SPIRIT. FOR THE SPIRIT SEARCHES ALL
THINGS, YES, THE DEEP THINGS OF GOD.
—1 CORINTHIANS 2:9–10

For years, my desire has been to pursue the knowledge of the Lord. I want to understand the things of God in a deeper way. Many times I have personalized 1 Corinthians 2:9–10 and prayed it over and over: "God, let my eyes see, let my ears hear that which You have prepared for me. Send Your Spirit to reveal the deep things of Your heart to me. What are you thinking? What are Your thoughts toward me, toward my family, and for this nation? Spirit of God, reveal what my mind cannot understand on its own."

God is beyond demonstration or definition. Our human minds cannot fully understand Him. Yet He longs for us to know Him, and so He has made a way for us to know Him by giving us the Holy Spirit. The knowledge of God is within the reach of even the weakest among us with the Spirit's guidance. The Spirit searches out the deepest parts of the Godhead and then reveals to us what He finds.

I imagine the knowledge of God as a vast ocean. The Holy Spirit is like a giant searchlight shining into that ocean to reveal God to us: His character, His attributes, His emotions, and mysteries hidden away since the foundation of the Earth. The Spirit reveals to us what our natural minds could never comprehend on their own. As we explore the knowledge of God, He guides us deeper until, suddenly, we see a glimmer of revelation. Each glimpse given to us enlightens our understanding to the glad heart of God and the passionate joy of Jesus Christ.

This revelation comes as we join with the Spirit in various ways. Sometimes He meets us as we study and meditate on the Word, serve others, pray, and work with an excellent spirit. Other times He meets us in dreams, as He met Jacob, Solomon, Daniel, Joseph, and many others in the Bible. All are opportunities to give ourselves fully to the Lord. For just as the Holy Spirit searches out the Godhead and reveals hidden things to us, He is simultaneously searching out the deepest parts of us and revealing our hidden thoughts and motives to God. As we say, "God, I want more of You in my life," God's answer to us is, "Yes, you can have more of Me, but I want more of you."

Revelation 4 is a powerful picture of surrender and heavenly humility. The twenty-four elders encircling the Lord's throne continually cast their crowns—their worth and all that they are—before the eternal God. They go low before Him, bowing down over and over.

This reality is not for them alone. God wants to make us great on the inside, bringing us into our eternal spiritual identity as humble worshipers of Him. The Lord is giving us an open invitation to join the elders in humbling ourselves before Him.

> AFTER THESE THINGS I LOOKED, AND BEHOLD, A DOOR STANDING OPEN IN HEAVEN. AND THE FIRST VOICE WHICH I HEARD WAS LIKE A TRUMPET SPEAKING WITH ME, SAYING, "COME UP HERE, AND I WILL SHOW YOU THINGS WHICH MUST TAKE PLACE AFTER THIS."
> —REVELATION 4:1

So how do we respond to this open door? We must realize that it is an opportunity for us to seek to understand God's heart and to walk humbly in all seasons of our lives. God is asking for humility to reign in the hearts of His people; by this we will show Jesus Christ as glorious as He truly is. He is asking us to go low like the elders.

## INVITATION TO ENCOUNTER

I have given myself to seeking God, and in the process I have had many dreams. I wanted to share these dreams because they are not just personal dreams; they are open to whomever has ears to hear. I believe they contain truths from the Lord for the entire Church and an invitation for all believers. As you read, put yourself into these dreams and let the Holy Spirit draw you into encounter.

The truths spoken in these dreams give us vivid pictures of how the Lord sees all believers and what He desires from each of us. He is looking for friends who will hear His invitation and go on the journey of humility before Him—those who will intercede with Him and who will love Him regardless of their life circumstances or position. If you set your heart to take this journey with the Lord, no matter what positions you may hold in life, He will meet you.

As you read through these dreams, keep a few things in mind. First, God promotes and demotes, and everything is backward in His Kingdom. He moves one to the front and another to the back. He loves them both the same, but He is fashioning their hearts to love Him fully regardless of the position they hold. In every season of our lives, God is looking for the heart that is abandoned to loving Him, whether we are shining in the front or hidden in the back. We can find great joy in being at the back of the line and even in being demoted, for we are strengthened and we encounter the Lord in those times. At other times, God invites us into a night season, asking us to love Him and trust that He will be with us throughout difficult seasons. Everything that happens to us must truly come through God first, and if it comes through God, He has a purpose in it: through each circumstance, He is again inviting us to love Him wholeheartedly. God is looking for those who love in every season and are faithfully devoted to Him, through pain and through success.

Second, we move God's heart when we are faithful in what little we are given. God helps us climb the mountain of holiness one step at a time; He is with us, for us, cheering us on and enjoying us every step of our journey. No one is held at bay or left out of this invitation. Even if we will never hold positions of authority or be famous, we can all be faithful with the responsibilities He has given us.

Lastly, every dream and every sentence is written in hopes that you will pray. Prayer is the simplest thing in the world to do, but it is the thing that is done the least. As a general definition, prayer is agreeing with God. Prayer is one of the primary ways we encounter Him, which leads to becoming like Him. The humble King greatly desires our partnership in agreeing with His heart.

I trust this describes you, so join me in a journey into understanding God's heart toward us. Sit with the Lord, hear His voice and let Him hear yours. As we seek Him, bow low in humility and cultivate an unoffended heart at every step, we will wait for Him to pour out His Spirit in astonishing ways.

> AND IT SHALL COME TO PASS IN THE LAST DAYS, SAYS GOD, THAT I WILL POUR OUT OF MY SPIRIT ON ALL FLESH; YOUR SONS AND YOUR DAUGHTERS SHALL PROPHESY, YOUR YOUNG MEN SHALL SEE VISIONS, YOUR OLD MEN SHALL DREAM DREAMS. AND ON MY MENSERVANTS AND ON MY MAIDSERVANTS I WILL POUR OUT MY SPIRIT IN THOSE DAYS; AND THEY SHALL PROPHESY.
> —ACTS 2:17–18

No matter what season **WE** are in, the *Lord* is {watching} to see what is in the depths of **OUR** soul. *He* wants **US** totally {empty} of **OURSELVES** so *He* can fill **US** with the {fullness} of the knowledge of *Him*. It is *His* passion and joy to {destroy} selfish ambition and pride in **US**.

# 1. Humility: The Pathway to Encounter

HUMBLE YOURSELVES IN THE SIGHT OF THE LORD AND
HE WILL LIFT YOU UP.
—JAMES 4:10

What does it mean to encounter God? Is it only when Jesus appears right in front of our eyes? Can anyone encounter the Lord, or are encounters reserved for those who have positions up front, such as pastors and leaders?

When you encounter someone, you come upon or meet the person. Encounter may be hoped for and desired, but it is unplanned, unexpected, or brief. Encountering God is like that. We cannot force God to meet with us or limit Him. He comes to those He wishes to meet, regardless of their position, in any way He wants. So many people get frustrated because they're looking for Jesus to appear to them face to face, and they refuse to acknowledge anything less. We miss many simple encounters when the Spirit of the Lord is speaking to us or directing us.

For years I wanted to supernaturally meet God. I wanted to experience Him in a very real and tangible way. I always loved hearing conference speakers relate their encounters with the Lord and how they would be taken up to heavenly places. They would see angels. They would speak to the Lord. I longed for all of that. I would ask God, "Why not me?"

I loved reading the scriptures about encountering the Lord. I would read them time and again. I would pray them. I wanted to know the mysteries of His heart for us, His thoughts toward us, and the secrets He holds. I figured I could never go wrong if I prayed His Word, so I would pray Revelation 4:1 over and over again.

> WE CANNOT FORCE GOD TO MEET WITH US OR LIMIT HIM. HE COMES TO THOSE HE WISHES TO MEET, REGARDLESS OF THEIR POSITION, IN ANY WAY HE WANTS.

After these things I looked, and behold, a door standing open in heaven. And the first voice which I heard was like a trumpet speaking with me, saying, "Come up here, and I will show you things which must take place after this."

There is a door open in Heaven and there is an invitation to come up and encounter God. This is not an order from an unfeeling, uninvolved father or a command from an emotionless superior, but an invitation from someone who embodies desire. And it is more than an invitation to simply come; it is an invitation to come *up*, to ascend. The Greek word for "come" is *anabaino*. It is not a one-time action, so it carries a lot of weight. *Anabaino* means to approach, to attain, and to be lifted up, and the word carries the idea of doing it continually. "Repetitive attainment with intensity" might be a good way to say it. The door is open in Heaven for us to come up and keep coming. We do not have to beg God to open the door or to let us come. The door is wide open—almost as if it were not able to close—and the invitation is already in our hands. Our task is to reach.

I knew this scripture that I had prayed often had been given to the Apostle John, but one day, as we were singing this scripture at the International House of Prayer in Kansas City (IHOP-KC), I felt a shift happen in my heart. After singing the verse a few times, I began to personalize it for myself. "There is an open door for *me*. *I* will come up."

Something deep inside my soul cried out, "This is for me. I want this encounter. I want to go up. I will not stop asking. Whatever I must do to get through this door, take me, God. I am Yours." From that moment, I began praying this verse from Revelation many times each day. Whenever my eyes opened, whether it was in the middle of the night or the next morning, this prayer was the first thing out of my mouth, week after week for months on end.

Little did I realize that the Lord would lead me to this open door through one specific pathway: the pathway of humility. Having humility means so much more than going as low as you can. It means embracing the lowest place and finding great joy there—in the last place, in the place of demotion and in the place of being overlooked.

Humility: this word embodied the Man Jesus when He walked the earth. Humility is the place of great encounter with Him, and it was my pathway to the door standing open in Heaven.

## FINDING JOY IN THE BACK ROW

I first encountered the Lord on the back row, in the midst of my anger, right after being demoted from my position as a worship leader. I didn't encounter Him in a prayer line, at a conference or amidst a tangible swirl of divine activity. No one was praying for me, I didn't see any angels, and I didn't hear any songs from Heaven. It was just the Spirit of the Lord quietly speaking to me as I sat on the back row, enraged at being removed from my position. The doors of Heaven were not thrown wide open for me; instead, He gave me a simple invitation to go on a step-by-step journey in humility.

I was already an experienced worship leader and singer by the time I had come to IHOP–KC. I had led worship and taught at several conferences around the nation, and I was comfortable in my worship style. In the early days of IHOP–KC, we were pioneering a new way to flow together as a team when singing prophetic songs. I struggled with the new style at first. I did my own thing. I didn't like change. A good friend eventually took me aside and said, "You know, Michael Jordan was always a great basketball player. But the Chicago Bulls really started winning when he learned to play with his team." However, I still continued to do my own thing.

One evening, I was leading worship. The next day, one of the leaders asked me to step down from the worship-leading rotation for a season, because I didn't involve others in the prophetic singing when I led. I was still allowed to sing on a team but not lead. He wanted me to take some time to learn the worship model. In fact, though he did not know it, the Lord was using him to teach me a valuable lesson in humility.

I must be honest and say I didn't take the news of my demotion well. In fact, I was furious. As I sat in the very back row during a worship set I should have been leading, my heart was seething and my mind was racing a hundred miles a minute. I frantically defended myself with irate whispers, muttering to myself, "I am Julie Meyer! I should not be on the back row. I was made for the front." Each time I would think these thoughts, the words would get louder and louder until I was uncontrollably mad, jealous, envious and frustrated—all the Christian words for angry. And it was all happening right in the middle of worship. Everything I should not be was at the forefront of my heart. I was not enjoying my new position on the back row one bit.

HUMILITY MEANS EMBRACING THE LOWEST PLACE AND FINDING GREAT JOY THERE—IN THE LAST PLACE, IN THE PLACE OF DEMOTION AND IN THE PLACE OF BEING OVERLOOKED.

I had read one of Bob Sorge's books, entitled *Dealing with the Rejection and Praise of Man*, and yet there I was . . . angry about what I saw as rejection. I wanted to be in the front; I *deserved* to be there. As the incense of worship was rising to God, I was yelling at Him on the inside, "I hate the back row! I hate the back row!"

People were walking by me and leaning down to ask, "Julie, why are you in the back? Aren't you supposed to be leading right now?" I would look up at them, shrug my shoulders and give them a huge, fake smile, while inside I was still yelling, "I hate the back row! Hate it, hate it, hate it!" I had a smile on my face, but I was an exploding volcano on the inside. I was fooling everyone but God Almighty, who sees and knows all (Psalm 139:1-4).

I still remember the worship song being played by the team

that took my spot. "Holy, holy are You, Lord God Almighty. Worthy is the Lamb. Worthy is the Lamb." God, at that exact moment, was getting ready to grace me with the encounter of a lifetime, but I was only focused on me.

All of a sudden—in the midst of my anger, envy, jealousy, pride and just about every other emotion contrary to the Sermon on the Mount lifestyle I sang about daily and professed to live—an interior whisper broke my concentration.

"I have an idea."

It was piercing, yet gentle. It was tender, yet it arrested my attention. The beautiful inner voice of the Holy Spirit, even in this place, did not condemn me, but repeated His invitation for me to dialogue with Him: "I have an idea." I remember responding, "Go on . . . "

"Every time you feel the sting that you are feeling now, embrace it and lean into My goodness. Do not get mad. Trust Me in this place; encounter Me in this place; be lovesick for Me in this place. I will either open the door for you to lead worship again or bring you into something else that you will enjoy just as much."

I sat there and thought about this for a minute. I was so focused on being mad, I didn't even realize I was having an intimate conversation with the Holy Spirit. In my pride and jealousy, the ever-wooing Holy Spirit was leading my prideful heart straight into the heart of God. It still surprises me when I say this, but I was encountering the Lord right in the middle of my temper tantrum.

I remember thinking to myself, "Okay, I am going to do this, but I won't tell anyone. I'll see if it works first. Every time I feel the sting of jealousy and the anger of being overlooked or demoted, I am going to lean into the sting. I am going to love

Jesus right in the midst of the sting. I am going to set my heart to find Him when I hurt the most."

I decided there on the back row (literally) to set my heart to find God and to find the joy of the Lord in the lowest place. I guessed that it was not going to be a short season—that it would take a year or two at the very least—but I decided to accept the invitation anyway. God was inviting me to spend some focused time with Him and I wanted to see what He was going to do in my life. So I began a step-by-step journey with Him into humility. Now that I had taken the first step, I would be invited to take another, then another. I would never know what the next thing was going to be until after I had taken a step.

I knew this journey would not be easy. I never imagined there could be any true joy in the lowest place. I thought joy only happened in the highest places of life, where everything was wonderful, everyone was your friend, and you led worship, preached or prophesied. Joy comes during good times, or at least that's what I thought. Finding joy on the back row was new to me. But it sure seems that God can do the deepest and greatest work on the inside when He tucks us away underneath the shadow of His wings. I'm sure that on the outside, it didn't look like much was happening, but that was certainly the time in my life when I felt the most change.

God loves to show us what is really in our hearts. So, how do we get to see it? Well, when life is normal, when there's nothing amazing or terrible happening, we are pretty settled; that's when we get to coast through our day. But when the mixture within our heart is shaken up and unsettled, our real thoughts, feelings and beliefs tend to rise to the surface. Many times this happens by demotion, getting fired, being overlooked or having no favor while everyone else seems to get all the awards. While your friends were invited to the pastors' luncheon, you were put on the bathroom cleaning crew. While your friends were invited to God's banquet feast, your invitation takes you straight into the dark night of the soul. This is the sting I'm talking about. This is the place of encounter with the living God.

> THE KINDEST VOICE TO EVER SPEAK TO MY HEART WAS THE HOLY SPIRIT BECKONING ME TO SEARCH OUT THE GOODNESS OF GOD IN HUMILITY

God's purpose is to make us great in Him, not just great for the sake of being great (John 15:1–17). I have realized that if you are called by God, especially into a leadership position, your training will come in the form of being overlooked, demoted, fired and having seasons of absolutely no favor at all (Proverbs 3:11–12, 13:24; Hebrews 12:1–11). But if you go low, the place of encountering the affections and the secrets of God's heart is right in the middle of the sting—at the end of the line and in the back row.

God knows everything, even down to the moments when we sit and stand back up again. Every single thing we do or think or say—yes, that includes the secret motives and hidden thoughts we can keep from those around us—He knows all of it. The grumbling, complaining and temper tantrums don't just dissolve somewhere in the atmosphere (Psalm 139:3–5).

The Spirit of mercy and kindness broke into my life that night in January of 2000. In the middle of my total weakness, envy and anger, He fully wanted an encounter with me. That fact was shocking and alluring all at once. But know this: the kindest voice to ever speak to my heart was the Holy Spirit beckoning me to search out the goodness of God in humility.

In the years since then, this lesson has come back to me a thousand times and it is never easy. A sting always does *sting*. It always feels personal. It always costs you something. But each time I feel that sting, I know what I should do: lean into Jesus and go low.

How will your heart react when everyone around is given honor, respect and position while you are ignored? Will you get offended? Will you call a leadership meeting to demand honor? Will you send an e-mail to the person who can change the situation for you? Will you complain to your friends instead of asking them to pray for you? Will you try to clear your name or show others your side of the story? Will you talk badly about other people's character and motives? Will you hope to win everyone who talks with you to your side? Will you let your hurt and anger justify some kind of retaliation? Our heart should be heavy if these things are true. The weight of what is staring back at us in the mirror should make us want to lean into God and ask for His strength.

## EXALTATION COMES FROM THE LORD

Though I had said yes to the Holy Spirit's invitation, I still was having trouble working through all the emotions of being fired by my friend and pastor. One day I came across this scripture.

> FOR EXALTATION COMES NEITHER FROM THE EAST NOR FROM THE WEST NOR FROM THE SOUTH. BUT GOD IS THE JUDGE: HE PUTS DOWN ONE, AND EXALTS ANOTHER.
> —PSALM 75:6-7

I felt like the Holy Spirit was yelling it at me. Man does not set us in our place; the Lord does. God raises up one and removes another (Daniel 2:20–21). God knows what is in our hearts, and wants us to see what He already knows . . . that most of us need a lot of help in going low and embracing the lowest place with joy. Of course the Lord uses others to affect our position, but the result is still the same; He is the one moving us. So it wasn't mainly about what someone else did to me, it was about recognizing God's hand in the midst of my circumstances and responding to His invitation.

Experiencing God's favor can be like riding a Ferris wheel. One minute you are up in the light of divine favor and the next you are down in the depths of the shadow. God wants us to find joy in both places. He wants us walking steady when we are up and walking steady when we are down. We should not focus on our position; no matter where we are, even if we are totally out of sight from everyone, God knows how to promote us and how to demote us.

> EXPERIENCING GOD'S FAVOR CAN BE LIKE RIDING A FERRIS WHEEL. ONE MINUTE YOU ARE UP IN THE LIGHT OF DIVINE FAVOR AND THE NEXT YOU ARE DOWN IN THE DEPTHS OF THE SHADOW.

I believe God trains us for greatness the same way He trained King David. Early on, we hear of David tending sheep in the boondocks of Bethlehem. But God whispers a secret about him in 1 Samuel 13:14: "The LORD has sought for Himself a man after His own heart, and the LORD has commanded him to be commander over His people."

From tending sheep to becoming the King of Israel, from killing Goliath to being hated and hunted by Saul and his massive army, from reigning in royalty to running for his life time and again, David was constantly on the favor Ferris wheel.

Throughout his songs and the stories told about him, we are taken with him every step of the way as he shares his deepest thoughts and groans about life and God. He was promoted to the highest heights and demoted to the lowest lows, but at the end of the day, what kept David's heart steady was how intently he focused on the Lord—he made the Lord his one thing.

> ONE THING I HAVE DESIRED OF THE LORD, THAT WILL I SEEK: THAT I MAY DWELL IN THE HOUSE OF THE LORD ALL THE DAYS OF MY LIFE, TO BEHOLD THE BEAUTY OF THE LORD, AND TO INQUIRE IN HIS TEMPLE.
> —PSALM 27:4

God took David on a journey of great sorrow and joy to learn how to embrace the highest and the lowest places while keeping his heart steady. This is the same journey God has us all on and, at the end of the day, the Lord's desire is that the cry of our heart would be the same: to be focused on God, our one thing.

When we are stuck in the low places, joy is not easily faked. In fact, the more we try to fake it, the more phony we become in the long run because our spirit will start to wither. For a while we might be able to pretend around our friends, family, ministry staff or coworkers, but we cannot pretend with God. "For the eyes of the LORD run to and fro throughout the whole earth, to show Himself strong on behalf of those whose heart is loyal to Him," and God knows the intentions of the heart (2 Chronicles 16:9; Jeremiah 17:10). God is actively looking for those whose hearts belong solely to Him during times of crushing and demotion (Psalm 62:5–12).

Sometimes it is hard to discern His invitation when our life circumstances are very difficult. We may experience loss, rejection, illness, and other hardships. But God promises us that He will never leave us nor forsake us, and His invitation is still open: to respond to Him with hearts that are unoffended, even in the midst of great pain. He will take us through the valley of the shadow hand in hand; He will be with us every step of the way (Psalm 23:4). Like Paul, we can desire to know Christ in all seasons: "that I may know Him and the power of His resurrection, and the fellowship of His sufferings . . . " (Philippians 3:10).

No matter what season we are in, the Lord is watching to see what is in the depths of our soul. He wants our soul to cling to Him and allow His right hand to uphold us (Psalm 63:8). He wants us totally empty of ourselves so He can fill us with the fullness of the knowledge of Him. It is His passion and joy to destroy selfish ambition and pride in us.

Here is the invitation from the Lord: if you want to go up, you have to go low; you have to join Him in understanding the power residing in the lowest place. He left the glory of Heaven and clothed Himself in skin forever. Jesus described Himself as meek and lowly (Matthew 11:29). He walked in humility when He was on the Earth and, according to Psalm 45, humility is one of the main causes He will take up when He returns. He is not going to look like the reserved child who came the first time, and He will not fulfill the role of the sacrificial Lamb again. The Lion of Judah will have fire in His eyes as He rides forth on behalf of truth, righteousness and humility when we see Him next.

> AND IN YOUR MAJESTY RIDE ON TRIUMPHANTLY FOR THE CAUSE OF TRUTH, HUMILITY, AND RIGHTEOUSNESS . . . AND LET YOUR RIGHT HAND GUIDE YOU TO TREMENDOUS THINGS.
> —PSALM 45:4, AMPLIFIED BIBLE; PARENTHETICAL COMMENT ADDED

Although not everyone may meet God in exactly the same way I did, this journey was not only for me; I believe He is extending His invitation for all of us to embrace every season in which we find ourselves. Sing for joy in the midst of promotion and sing for joy in demotion—when you are alone in your bed, when no one is looking and it is just you and God alone. No matter what your journey, let it be your invitation to encounter.

> LET THE SAINTS BE JOYFUL IN GLORY; LET THEM SING
> ALOUD ON THEIR BEDS.
> —PSALM 149:5

Let His kind eyes
WASH you
from the inside out and let
His MERCY
surround you.
*Jesus* wants to share His
{secrets}
with His friends,
and here is the {key}:
*come* and *sit* awhile.

# 2. Come and Sit Awhile

I LOVE THIS DREAM BECAUSE IT IS AN INVITATION TO ALL
OF US TO COME AND SIT AWHILE WITH THE KING OF THE
AGES. LET HIS KIND EYES WASH YOU FROM THE INSIDE
OUT AND LET HIS MERCY SURROUND YOU. JESUS WANTS
TO SHARE HIS SECRETS WITH HIS FRIENDS, AND HERE IS
THE KEY: COME AND SIT AWHILE.

I had a dream. I was sound asleep when I felt someone tap me on the shoulder and wake me up. When
I sat up, I saw a man on my left side pointing to the
other side of the bed.

I looked to the right and saw Jesus sitting at a round table
with an extra chair. He pointed to it and extended an invitation to me: "Come and sit awhile."

> WHILE THE KING IS AT HIS TABLE, MY SPIKENARD (MY LIFE
> AND WORSHIP) SENDS FORTH ITS FRAGRANCE.
> —SONG OF SOLOMON 1:12; PARENTHETICAL COMMENT
> ADDED

I walked over to the table and sat down. I remember noticing
how His eyes never left my face. He watched every step I took.

He had an old book in front of Him. This book was large and thick, and it looked like worn brown leather. It would have been almost square if not for its constant use. The Lord was touching the cover very tenderly and running His fingers around the edges, like the book was dear to Him. It reminded me of the moments during family reunions when the photos of generations past are brought out to show the younger generation. The elders turn the pages carefully, not because the photo albums are old, but because the pictures are precious.

IN ONE GLANCE, I FELT DEEP CONVICTION. IN ONE GLANCE, AN OVERWHELMING FLOOD OF MERCY AND DELIGHT AWAKENED MY HEART.

For some time I watched Jesus' face, His countenance full of unspoken emotion, as He touched the front of this cherished book. He knew what was in it and was clearly moved. He looked into my eyes and again said, "Come and sit awhile."

He was intent on looking straight into my eyes, and I couldn't look away from His gaze. I was drawn in by Him; everything I had carefully hidden away was opened with one glance.

His eyes were shining. The eyes of the Lord looked straight into my soul and caused everything to be laid bare. His gaze is where joy and peace give an open invitation into their home; where all of my hidden sins and hidden places are brought into the light and there is no hiding at all; where I finally understand His love and desire for me—I was drawn in by *those* eyes.

In one glance, I felt deep conviction. In one glance, an overwhelming flood of mercy and delight awakened my heart. In one glance, conviction and mercy met and entwined themselves with each other, causing me to want to run straight to Him as fast as I could and lean into Him. Again He said, "Come and sit awhile."

The King of creation was at a table with me, like He had nothing else to do but sit and just be . . . with me.

When Jesus looked back down at the book, I noticed that it had a title. He turned it for me to read.

### Hidden Secrets of the Ages: Past, Present and What Is To Come

I looked up into His eyes, and He nodded at me to open it. I could feel the tiny ridges and grooves of the old leather as I touched it. I lifted the heavy cover and glanced at a couple of the chapters. The first one I saw was called, "The End from the Beginning," and right underneath the title were the words, "Come and Sit Awhile." I kept reading.

### THINGS YET TO BE REVEALED
### *Come and Sit Awhile*

### WALKING DOWN THE ANCIENT PATHS
### *Come and Sit Awhile*

### 2 KINGS 6:12
### *Come and Sit Awhile*

There were many more chapters, but the Lord reached out His hand, closed the book and said, "Let's just sit awhile. Let's just sit and know." And we sat there for the rest of the dream. He just sat with me all night.

When I woke up in the morning I knew that I had been with the King at His table all night long.

We move {Heaven} when
*God* stirs our heart

to PR*AY* **DAY AND NIGHT.**

When we entwine ourselves

with *His purposes* and

are faithful to the

{invitation} to **INTERCEDE,**

*He acts* on behalf of those

who **WAIT** for Him.

# 3. I Am Undone

WE MOVE HEAVEN WHEN GOD STIRS OUR HEART TO
PRAY DAY AND NIGHT (ISAIAH 62). WHEN WE ENTWINE
OURSELVES WITH HIS PURPOSES AND ARE FAITHFUL TO
THE INVITATION TO INTERCEDE, HE ACTS ON BEHALF OF
THOSE WHO WAIT FOR HIM. THIS DREAM IS A PICTURE
ABOUT HOW FAITHFULNESS, ESPECIALLY IN INTERCES-
SION, MOVES GOD'S HEART (PSALM 132:3-5).

I had a dream. An angel took me into the room of a man who was deep in sleep. We stood together at the foot of his bed so the angel could show me how this faithful person spent even his unconscious hours. I could hear the man praying while he was asleep. Every time he would roll over in his bed, he would say, "Abba, here I am. Here I am, Abba. I love You, Abba."

I looked up through the ceiling and saw a vast angelic army. Together the angels seemed like an ocean of brilliant, radiant light. It appeared that they were pulsing and trembling, just waiting to break in. They were waiting to be released by the call of the angel who had led me into the room. He was in great anguish because he earnestly desired to give the call they were all expecting, but he only said one sentence: "It is not quite time yet."

I kept looking at the heavenly hosts. I could see ladders. I could see lamps. I could feel the anticipation and how strongly they wanted to break in. The angelic multitude was getting ready to burst in, not with a simple entrance, but with a flood of divine activity. Only this single angel held back the imminent breakthrough.

But it was not quite time for him to release them. There was something yet to be completed before the breakthrough could happen, though I was not shown what it was.

I noticed the Lord standing at the head of the man's bed. I was able to feel His gaze of tender kindness and hear His gentle whisper over the man. He said, "So many people said they would do it, and they never did, but you really did it. You really did it." The Lord's affirming voice, affection and kindness to the man were due to the man's faithfulness in continual night and day prayer, even in the mundane things of life. This man did not seek fame and fortune; he stayed steady, lovesick for God and unoffended day by day.

> THE ANGELIC MULTITUDE WAS GETTING READY TO BURST IN, NOT WITH A SIMPLE ENTRANCE, BUT WITH A FLOOD OF DIVINE ACTIVITY.

A tear came from the corner of the Lord's eye; He was deeply moved by this man's faithfulness. The tear fell in slow motion and broke into a hundred tiny splashes on the man's pillow. It was beautiful to watch. This display of passion was a side of the Lord I had not seen before.

From my vantage point, I noticed that the man's room

was as bright as day even in the darkness, because the hosts of Heaven were so close to breaking through. The Lord looked at me and said, "We have heard many pray, 'Take us up.' Instead, tell the faithful ones, 'Heaven is coming down. Heaven is breaking in.'"

The Lord added, "And tell them, I am undone."

Oh, the *beauty* of the {myrrh}— the {prayers} of the **SAINTS** for healing! It is so *beautiful* and it is so **POWERFUL**.

# 4. The Beauty of the Myrrh

I HAD A DREAM ABOUT A WONDERFUL WOMAN IN OUR MIDST NAMED MARY. WHILE MANY IN OUR COMMUNITY AND AROUND THE WORLD WERE CRYING OUT TO THE LORD FOR HER HEALING FROM CANCER, JESUS TOOK HER HOME; SHE WAS HEALED AS SHE STEPPED INTO ETERNITY. I FELT LIKE JESUS OPENED THE DOOR IN A NEW WAY SO WE COULD SEE THE POWER OF PRAYER FROM AN ETERNAL PERSPECTIVE. SOMETIMES OUR PRAYERS SEEM TO GO UNANSWERED, BUT THEY ASCEND TO THE HEAVENS WHERE HE HEARS EVERY SINGLE ONE; HE BENDS DOWN TO LISTEN. PSALM 116:1-2 SAYS, "I LOVE THE LORD, BECAUSE HE HAS HEARD MY VOICE AND MY SUPPLICATIONS. BECAUSE HE HAS INCLINED HIS EAR TO ME, THEREFORE I WILL CALL UPON HIM AS LONG AS I LIVE." MAYBE YOU HAVE SOMEONE LIKE MARY IN YOUR LIFE . . . WHILE YOU WERE PRAYING FOR THEIR HEALING, GOD TOOK THEM HOME. THE LORD ASSURED ME, "IN A MINUTE YOU WILL SEE THEM AGAIN, AND THIS DARK NIGHT IS ACTUALLY FILLING THE BOWLS THAT JESUS CHRIST WILL POUR OUT ON THE EARTH." OH, THE BEAUTY OF THE MYRRH—THE PRAYERS OF THE SAINTS FOR HEALING! IT IS SO BEAUTIFUL AND IT IS SO POWERFUL.

I had a dream. I saw Jesus go into Mary's hospital room. It was dark in her room, so I knew it was the night hour (Song of Solomon 5:2). Mary was surrounded by her family. They were keeping watch over her and praying, but they could not see Jesus. He walked over to Mary and touched her hands. Her whole body was dripping with thick myrrh because her family had covered her in unoffended prayer.

As she sat up in her bed, it was like she sat up in an entirely different world . . . it was bright, colorful and radiant, and the myrrh on her body had vanished. She sat up glowing and smiling. All the while, Jesus just looked intently at her. They both looked at each other for a moment, and then Jesus turned away. Even without words, I knew I was looking at Song of Solomon 6:5, where Jesus says to His Bride, "Turn your eyes away from me, for they have overcome me."

With ease and quickness, Mary sprang up from her bed. She noticed that everything about her body was transformed and immediately knew she was in a different realm. She looked around the room at her family as Jesus quieted her heart with one whispered phrase: "You will see them all in just a minute." And Mary knew it was true.

For the first time, Mary had a deep understanding of how soon they would all see each other again (Psalm 90:4). To humans living on this side of time, the days seem long, but in eternity, those earthly days are numbered and seen for how short they truly are. Leaving her family would be like dropping her children off in the nursery when they were young. They cried because they were being separated, because they did not understand she would be back in an hour to pick them up. But she knew exactly when she would return. When Mary stepped into eternity, she had a new concept of time and she knew she would see them again—in just a minute.

They both stood there looking at her family. Mary was so tender and loving as she looked at them from the other side of time. Although they could not hear her, she said to them, "You did good. Well done." I knew she was referring to how they had handled her season of suffering without becoming offended at the Lord. She said to Jesus, "This is my family . . . just look at them. I am so proud of them." She had a look in her eyes that only a wife and a mom can have; she was overwhelmed with love for her family. She kept saying, "You did good. You did good."

The scene changed, and they both turned to face gently flowing waters and green fields. Mary began running and laughing. She was undeniably free. It was like she could not run fast enough. Her laughter filled the air as Jesus just stood there and watched her run.

With an excited sparkle in His bright eyes, Jesus said, "Come see." He led Mary by the hand into a giant room in the corridors of eternity. The room contained many bowls that had the appearance of enormous communion chalices. Each one seemed about fifty feet tall and very wide, with a large, sturdy base that tapered to form a stem. At the top of the stem was a bowl that was as wide as it was deep. The bowls were made of something clear, like glass or diamond, so it was easy to see how full they were from the outside. Some of the bowls had just a little liquid in them and some were about half full,

THE SEASON OF THE DARK NIGHT IS WORKING TO FILL THE BOWLS WITH PRAYERS FROM HEARTS AND THOUGHTS THAT ARE PURE, REFINED AND LOVESICK.

but each liquid had its own color and each bowl had its own purpose. The liquid represented intercession.

The room they were in was very loud. The prayers of the saints on Earth would echo in this corridor until they came to rest in the bowls as unified, purified liquid prayers (Revelation 5:8).

Jesus took Mary to a bowl specifically for healing. When she saw how much liquid was in the bowl, she asked, "What is that?"

"This is liquid myrrh," He answered. The spice was the color of pure gold, like a thick, golden lava, and it almost ran over the top of the bowl.

Jesus explained, "It is the prayers of the saints for healing. As the saints were praying for healing for you and for many others, their hearts and minds were set to love Me. To the same degree that they leaned into the goodness of the Lord amidst their dark times, their thoughts and prayers were being refined by the fire. They learned how to not be offended. Look, Mary, their prayers are ever before me—like pure liquid gold—and you had a part in the filling of the bowls.

"Mary, you went your way up the mountain. You said yes to Me even in a dark night, in a time of difficulty. And when an enemy of God invaded your body, you did not open your mouth in offense and anger. Only grace, trust and faith in the goodness of God proceeded from your mouth. So, for the way you lived when death met you face to face—for willingly laying down your life and leaning into Me without offense—I now give you a crown of honor."

He placed the crown on her head. Then Jesus said, "Mary, watch." He tipped one of the gigantic bowls a little so that some of the golden liquid fell to Earth. As it fell, a special joy took hold of Mary; she clapped her hands, laughed and was so excited because she knew it meant good things.

They bent over and looked at Earth together. Great signs and wonders and great healings broke out in the places where the golden liquid fell. "I am giving them a taste," Jesus said, "but the day is coming when the bowls will be fully tipped over and poured out upon the earth."

As she stood looking at the bowl of myrrh, Jesus said, "Mary, you are one of the reasons this bowl is so full. The season of the dark night is working to fill the bowls with prayers from hearts and thoughts that are pure, refined and lovesick. When prayers come before Me that are full of demands and offense, they do not fill the bowls. But look how full the bowl is with the beauty of the myrrh. This is so beautiful and this is so powerful! The way you lived and the way you left the Earth has caused saints from many nations to lean into Me and pray out of lovesickness without offense . . . and look, Mary. Look how full the bowl is."

*God* is looking at
the {hidden motives} of
our heart and thoughts.
He wants us to go
to the LOWEST PLACE
and *embrace*
{true humility}—and to
**FULLY DELIGHT** in it. These
are the ones on whom He
*shines* His {light of favor}
and gives *promotion*.

# 5. Pink Slips

GOD IS LOOKING AT THE HIDDEN MOTIVES OF OUR HEART AND THOUGHTS. HE WANTS US TO GO TO THE LOWEST PLACE AND EMBRACE TRUE HUMILITY—AND TO FULLY DELIGHT IN IT. THESE ARE THE ONES ON WHOM HE SHINES HIS LIGHT OF FAVOR AND GIVES PROMOTION. HE KNOWS EXACTLY HOW OUR HEART RESPONDS WHEN WE ARE STUCK ON THE BACK ROW OR IN THE LOWEST PLACES.

AND HE SAT DOWN, CALLED THE TWELVE, AND SAID TO THEM, "IF ANYONE DESIRES TO BE FIRST, HE SHALL BE LAST OF ALL AND SERVANT OF ALL." —MARK 9:35

BUT WHEN YOU ARE INVITED, GO AND SIT DOWN IN THE LOWEST PLACE, SO THAT WHEN HE WHO INVITED YOU COMES HE MAY SAY TO YOU, "FRIEND, GO UP HIGHER." THEN YOU WILL HAVE GLORY IN THE PRESENCE OF THOSE WHO SIT AT THE TABLE WITH YOU. FOR WHOEVER EXALTS HIMSELF WILL BE HUMBLED, AND HE WHO HUMBLES HIMSELF WILL BE EXALTED.—LUKE 14:10–11

I had a dream. A man was sitting at his desk with a pile of phone messages in front of him. He represented the various genuine activities and movements the Lord was directing in the Body of Christ throughout the world. He was resting his head in his hands because he was overwhelmed with the incredible volume of messages awaiting his reply.

I saw some of the names on the messages. Certain ones were from people interested in forming partnerships with the movements they believed God was emphasizing in this season of history; there was no guile in them. Other messages were from people who only wanted to be able to say that their personal ministry was connected with something God was legitimately doing. All they wanted was fame and recognition. The overwhelmed man asked, "How will I know who to run with?"

"HE WHO FINDS DELIGHT IN THE LOWEST PLACE . . ."

I could see the Lord standing beside him with eyes like blazing fire, yet He answered with very simple, gentle statements.

"He who delights in the back of the line more than the front of the line."

"He who delights in being at the back table in the banquet room."

"He who finds delight in the lowest place."

Then the Lord said, "These are your comrades. These are the ones you will run with . . . and all the others will get their pink slips."

{Prophetic dreams} and
{prophetic words} are
never intended to be
a **GUARANTEE**.
Rather, they are
{invitations} to join
*Jesus Christ,*
the great *intercessor,*
in prayer for the **PURPOSES**
of *God* in the earth.

# 6. Saul of Tarsus

PROPHETIC DREAMS AND PROPHETIC WORDS ARE NEV-
ER INTENDED TO BE A GUARANTEE. RATHER, THEY ARE
INVITATIONS TO JOIN JESUS CHRIST, THE GREAT INTER-
CESSOR, IN PRAYER FOR THE PURPOSES OF GOD IN THE
EARTH. WHEN WE JOIN OUR PRAYERS FROM ALL OVER
THE WORLD WITH JESUS, CHANGE WILL COME AS HE
DISPLAYS HIS POWER AND SAVES TO THE UTTERMOST
(HEBREWS 7:25).

I had a dream. I was standing in the place of change
in Heaven. This place was like a council room. De-
cisions were made and requests were granted here
because of the intercession that rises to the Lord.

As I stood on the floor, I saw golden lava bubbling and
rising underneath me, and I knew it was an increase in intercession. The lava would rise through Heaven's floor, building up tension until it burst through the floor of the room to
touch the Father's heart—and suddenly, the Son would decree
*change*.

The scene changed and I was taken into an instance in history when intercession was at a high level. In my dream, I saw Saul before and during his conversion. The dream was like watching a movie unfolding, particularly focusing on what was happening with Saul. I knew I was seeing the earthly result of heavenly change.

> NOW SAUL WAS CONSENTING TO [STEPHEN'S] DEATH . . . THEN SAUL, STILL BREATHING THREATS AND MURDER AGAINST THE DISCIPLES OF THE LORD, WENT TO THE HIGH PRIEST AND ASKED LETTERS FROM HIM TO THE SYNAGOGUES OF DAMASCUS, SO THAT IF HE FOUND ANY WHO WERE OF THE WAY, WHETHER MEN OR WOMEN, HE MIGHT BRING THEM BOUND TO JERU-SALEM. AS HE JOURNEYED HE CAME NEAR DAMASCUS, AND SUDDENLY A LIGHT SHONE AROUND HIM FROM HEAVEN. THEN HE FELL TO THE GROUND, AND HEARD A VOICE SAYING TO HIM, "SAUL, SAUL, WHY ARE YOU PERSECUTING ME?" AND HE SAID, "WHO ARE YOU, LORD?" THEN THE LORD SAID, "I AM JESUS, WHOM YOU ARE PERSECUTING. IT IS HARD FOR YOU TO KICK AGAINST THE GOADS." SO HE, TREMBLING AND ASTON-ISHED, SAID, "LORD, WHAT DO YOU WANT ME TO DO?" THEN THE LORD SAID TO HIM, "ARISE AND GO INTO THE CITY, AND YOU WILL BE TOLD WHAT YOU MUST DO."
> —ACTS 8:1 AND 9:1-6

I could see Saul, driven by perfectionistic zeal, nodding his approval to Stephen's death with a little smirk on his face. I saw the bright light blazing all around as Saul fell to the ground. He fell hard, too. I saw the story unfold line by line, like it was happening again.

Then a thunderous voice abruptly said, "It is going to hap-pen again. There is a man who has set his heart against Me and My people Israel, but he is Mine. He is Mine. I am going to encounter him and turn his heart in one breath."

"And then . . . then . . . then . . ." The word *then* kept echoing and resounding through my head with a crescendo that grew increasingly sure.

"Then . . ." the voice said, "then Acts chapter 2 is going to happen all over again."

THE LAVA WOULD RISE THROUGH HEAVEN'S FLOOR, BUILDING UP TENSION UNTIL IT BURST THROUGH THE FLOOR OF THE ROOM TO TOUCH THE FATHER'S HEART.

This dream came to me many times, but each time Saul stood out to me. As the dream progressed, I saw the interaction between Saul and Ananias and how the Church did not believe Saul's conversion was genuine.

NOW THERE WAS A CERTAIN DISCIPLE AT DAMASCUS NAMED ANANIAS; AND TO HIM THE LORD SAID IN A VISION, "ANANIAS." AND HE SAID, "HERE I AM, LORD." SO THE LORD SAID TO HIM, "ARISE AND GO TO THE STREET CALLED STRAIGHT, AND INQUIRE AT THE HOUSE OF JUDAS FOR ONE CALLED SAUL OF TARSUS, FOR BEHOLD, HE IS PRAYING. AND IN A VISION HE HAS SEEN A MAN NAMED ANANIAS COMING IN AND PUTTING HIS HAND ON HIM, SO THAT HE MIGHT RECEIVE HIS SIGHT." THEN ANANIAS ANSWERED, "LORD, I HAVE HEARD FROM MANY ABOUT THIS MAN, HOW MUCH HARM HE HAS DONE TO YOUR SAINTS IN JERUSALEM. AND HERE HE HAS AUTHORITY FROM THE CHIEF PRIESTS TO BIND ALL WHO CALL ON YOUR NAME."
—ACTS 9:10–14

God did not show me who this modern-day Saul is, but I believe this person exists. In my dream, I remember thinking it was someone from the Middle East who currently is actively against God and Israel; it is a person who has a measure of authority or an amount of granted status.

In my dream, I saw the Lord bring this person into the Body of Christ, and it caused great controversy. But whenever and however this event happens, we are to know that the Lord is orchestrating this person's entire conversion. Until then, God has invited us to intercede until the Son decrees change.

The process of
{crushing} and {refining}
is often painful and difficult,

but if we **RESPOND**
in *acceptance*,
we will be the

**SWEET FRAGRANCE**
of *prayer*
to *Him*.

# 7. Becoming Fragrance

THE LORD WANTS US TO ASK HIM FOR MORE OF HIS PRESENCE, HIS SPIRIT AND HIS GIFTS, YET OFTEN WE ARE NOT READY FOR THEM; WE DO NOT UNDERSTAND WHAT WE ARE PRAYING FOR. THE LORD WANTS TO ANSWER OUR PRAYERS, BUT HE MUST PURIFY US FIRST— AND HIS REFINING OF US COMES FROM HIS PASSION FOR US. IN HIS MERCY AND LOVE, HE BRINGS MANY FORMS OF PRESSURE INTO OUR LIVES, WATCHING TO SEE WHAT WILL ARISE FROM OUR HEARTS IN RESPONSE. WHETHER THE SCENT IS A FRAGRANCE DEPENDS ON HOW WE REACT WHEN WE UNDERSTAND THAT MANY TIMES THESE PRESSURES ARE HIS ANSWER TO OUR PRAYERS. THE PROCESS OF CRUSHING AND REFINING IS OFTEN PAINFUL AND DIFFICULT, BUT IF WE RESPOND IN ACCEPTANCE, WE WILL BE THE SWEET FRAGRANCE OF PRAYER TO HIM.

I had a dream. In my dream, I woke up, got out of my bed and walked to where an angel was standing at the foot of the bed. The angel was so brilliant that it hurt my eyes to look at him. The angel said several times, "Pressure is coming. Pressure is coming."

I was shown a forge where silver is heated and purified by fire. I could feel the heat from the fire on my skin. Huge hands of a refiner were gently tending the silver in the extreme heat. I knew that the Refiner's hands were also the Potter's hands; the same hands which work the silver also mold the clay.

Suddenly, the scene changed and I was standing on the platform in a prayer room. In front of me was a huge boulder that had fallen through the roof. The Lord was standing beside the boulder, asking me, "Do you know what you ask for?" His voice was terrifying. It sounded like charging thunder, or like a huge wave about to crash down in the middle of a vast and resounding sea. He asked me again, "Do you know what you are asking for?" The power of His voice shook the whole room so much that I fell backwards.

THE SCULPTURE HAS ALREADY BEEN SIGNED BY THE GREAT POTTER HIMSELF. HE HAS MARKED HIS NAME ON THE CLAY.

His eyes were like an inferno. As He looked around at the people in the prayer room, representing believers everywhere, He saw into the deepest parts of our beings and knew our hearts completely. I felt the terrifying tension of His eyes piercing us—seeing right through us and exposing every flaw and weakness—but simultaneously calling us to become who He intended us to be. I felt Him saying, "It's yours; just ask for it. I have been waiting since the foundations of the earth for people to cry out for it. I have been waiting to give it all. It's *yours;* just ask." I knew He was referring to the fullness of our destiny in Him, the gifts and relationship that have always been available to anyone who pursues Him. He wants us to ask for our inheritance in Him.

Again the scene changed, and I knew I would be experiencing something directed at all those in the Church who were crying out for more of God. I found myself at the foot of a large table as a shower of bread crumbs fell from this table onto the floor. I knew I was in the parable of Matthew 15:25–28, in which Jesus tests the Canaanite woman's faith. I felt tremendous faith rise within me as I raced to grab each tumbling crumb. Jesus knew who He created His Church to be, but it is not enough for Jesus to say to us, "This is who you are." We have to believe it for ourselves. As I picked up the crumbs, I believed more and more in who Jesus said I was. Then the Lord said, "Woman, you have great faith."

I looked up and I could see the sky through the large hole in the roof. I saw a tremendous amount of brilliant white spots floating down toward the earth, so I thought it was snowing. But as the snow came nearer, I realized it was a throng of angels swarming by the hundreds into prayer rooms and churches across the world. This invasion of heavenly messengers and angelic activity steadily poured in through the open hole in the ceiling.

There were all kinds of angels with chariots and strong horses. Four mighty angels in chariots stationed themselves at all four corners of the building, standing guard over the people. They were warring angels and had a terrifying presence of authority.

Many of these brilliant messengers were dancing, some even in the air. Others had harps and were singing, "Hallelujah," and the sound of the music and the harmonies was like that of the largest, most entrancing choir I had ever heard. Some angels had paintbrushes and were painting bold colors on the ceiling, the walls, and in the air above people's heads.

Some angels had the sole mission of releasing the beauty of God. As they sang and danced, they scattered sparkling, tiny diamonds and sapphires all over the building. As the jewels came toward people, they would become lodged in their inner man—their soul, mind and heart. I saw some gems get planted in the area of the mind that receives understanding, while other gems came to rest on their heart. I reached up and caught one of the jewels. On it was written the word *understanding*. I reached up and caught another, which read *revelation*.

As these diamonds and sapphires were implanted, the people themselves would begin to shine with an inner glow, as if a great light had been turned on within them. The angels spun around in the air, loosing creativity and gifts of revelation; everything became imbued with vivid color, tangible beauty and transcendent music. The music, the voices and the sight of the angels eclipsed everything I have ever experienced in my life.

Suddenly, a mighty wind began to blow so hard that it knocked everyone to the ground. We were flat on the floor and could not get up—and it was amazing. All we could do was lie there and watch the angels continue in their activities. They rode the winds as they painted, sang and released more revelation of God's beauty.

Then came an abrupt, heavy rain like nothing I have ever seen; it seemed as if a dam had broken in the heavens and the water would fill the building before we could react. We struggled to our feet. In what seemed like a blink of an eye, we were up to our waist in water. I remember thinking we did not even have time to get used to the water being at our ankles; the water level came right to our waist almost immediately. The angels kept doing their work, but we were not ready to receive what we had been asking for because the answer had come so fast. We were not prepared for such a quick response from Heaven. We were caught off guard by the outpouring of the Spirit.

The scene changed, and again I was standing at the foot of my bed, watching the Lord tend the kiln with His huge hands. He intently watched the clay throughout every moment it took for the clay to be purified. There was such joy in the face of the Potter as He put pressure on the clay to make it into a beautiful sculpture. He had great joy in bringing pressure. He knew just what to do to make each part of the clay bend and fold. During this scene, I heard the angel say again, "Pressure is coming."

THE REFINING AND MOLD-ING BRINGS ABOUT A FRA-GRANCE THAT ASCENDS TO THE THRONE. IT ALL ASCENDS; EVERY PART OF HOW WE LIVE ASCENDS.

Refining is coming; the sculpting of an end-time people is coming. The sculpture has already been signed by the great potter Himself. He has marked His name on the clay.

I was shown the refining process from the perspective from Heaven, and I could see a vapor arising. As I looked down, I saw that it was coming from underneath the rock on the stage. The rising fragrance was like a valley full of wildflowers or a whole room filled with fresh roses. I looked up at the Lord. He was smiling as He said, "The unoffended prayers of the saints arise like sweet-smelling incense." Those who were not offended at God's refining process had offered up their prayers as a sweet fragrance that filled the corridors of Heaven.

I also saw black smoke arising that smelled like sulfur. The stench was produced by prayers that came from offense and anger. I realized that all prayers arise and that the Lord really hears them all. How we live arises before the Lord either like a sweet fragrance or a sulfuric stench, depending upon our heart response to His refining and molding process.

I looked at the Lord, who was basking in the fragrance of the sweet perfume arising from the saints. He was smiling as if He was surrounded by the most beautiful fragrance in existence. I knew I was seeing Song of Solomon Song 1:12 play out in front of me: while the King is at His table, our perfume spreads its fragrance.

Suddenly I was back in my room again, still smelling that most beautiful fragrance of the unoffended prayers. I could hear these words: "Remember this: the crushing brings about a fragrance that ascends to the Throne. The pressure brings about a fragrance that ascends to the Throne. The refining and molding brings about a fragrance that ascends to the Throne. It all ascends; every part of how we live ascends."

The Father's *kindness*
toward us is
so **GOOD**.
In His *mercy*,
He {trains} us to {run}
the race of **FAITH**
with *excellence* and
wants us to give up
**EVERYTHING** that
{hinders} us from
running well.

# 8. April Snow

THE FATHER'S KINDNESS TOWARD US IS SO GOOD. IN HIS MERCY, HE TRAINS US TO RUN THE RACE OF FAITH WITH EXCELLENCE AND WANTS US TO GIVE UP EVERYTHING THAT HINDERS US FROM RUNNING WELL. GOD REJOICES WHEN WE TEAR OUR HEARTS IN REPENTANCE AND LEAVE OUR SINS BEHIND (PHILIPPIANS 3:12–14). REPENTANCE IS AN ACT OF HUMILITY, LOVE AND SACRIFICE, AND IT TAKES MUCH HUMILITY TO EMBRACE RIGHTEOUSNESS. BUT IF WE WILL LEAN INTO OUR LOVING FATHER, HE WILL GIVE US GRACE AS ABUNDANT AS SOAKING RAIN.

*I* had a dream. This dream came the last week of February 2007, when the weather was unusually warm for Kansas City. Many people were already wearing flip-flop sandals and shorts. It was so warm that I decided I should get my spring and summer clothes out.

In the dream, the Lord said, "Do not take out your spring and summer clothes yet, for there is still more snow coming—behold, even into April. With every snowflake that falls to the ground, I want you to remember righteousness, righteousness, righteousness. With every snowflake that falls to the ground, remember purity, purity, purity."

I was taken and placed in the middle of a large training area full of many people. This part of the dream was a picture of the Bride being prepared. We wore white jerseys, as if we were ready to compete in the Olympics, but we were not clean.

My eyes were opened to see writing on each jersey describing that person's secret life. I could see selfish ambition written on some jerseys. I saw gossip on others. I saw grumbling and complaining—these sins were highlighted as big deals to God. Some people's jerseys were labeled with sexual sin: lustful thoughts, pornography, adultery and fornication. God was watching every hidden thing. Despite the secrets we kept to ourselves in darkness, He saw everything.

> EVEN THE NIGHT SHALL BE LIGHT ABOUT ME; INDEED,
> THE DARKNESS SHALL NOT HIDE FROM YOU, BUT THE
> NIGHT SHINES AS THE DAY; THE DARKNESS AND THE
> LIGHT ARE BOTH ALIKE TO YOU.
> —PSALM 139:11–12

The Lord appeared with a dual expression of His heart in the dream. He was at once the tender Father and the firm athletic coach. He had so much passion for us to become the greatest that He created us to be. He was training us because He was determined that we would win the race.

> NOT THAT I HAVE ALREADY ATTAINED, OR AM ALREADY
> PERFECTED; BUT I PRESS ON, THAT I MAY LAY HOLD OF
> THAT FOR WHICH CHRIST JESUS HAS ALSO LAID HOLD OF
> ME. BRETHREN, I DO NOT COUNT MYSELF TO HAVE AP-
> PREHENDED; BUT ONE THING I DO, FORGETTING THOSE

THINGS WHICH ARE BEHIND AND REACHING FORWARD
TO THOSE THINGS WHICH ARE AHEAD, I PRESS TOWARD
THE GOAL FOR THE PRIZE OF THE UPWARD CALL OF GOD
IN CHRIST JESUS.
—PHILIPPIANS 3:12–14

The Lord looked at us in our soiled jerseys with desire and determination. He was desirous of our affection and of our maturity, and He was determined about our future with Him. As a Father, He was full of love for us even in our weakness, but He did not want us to stay weak. He wanted us in the race. He was overjoyed with our choice to follow Him, even though He knew there was much work to be done. I could feel His fatherly heart and how He longed to take care of us. At the same time, His eyes were focused like a training coach. He was intent on preparing us. He cautioned us, saying, "You are not yet ready." And He intended to get us ready.

I PRESS TOWARD THE GOAL FOR THE PRIZE OF THE UPWARD CALL OF GOD IN CHRIST JESUS.

He showed me that there would be a season of intense rain in addition to the season of snow in Kansas City. I saw the rain saturate the ground. The Lord kept saying, "With every drop of rain that falls to the ground, I am sending grace upon grace to get you free from that which trips you up, from the sin that so easily entangles you. Remember grace."

The scripture highlighted to me was Hosea 6:1 and 3: "Come, and let us return to the LORD . . . He will come to us like the rain."

The scene changed, and I saw people standing in a line, waiting to pray publicly. One by one, they stepped forward and prayed the same thing from Isaiah 64:1: "Oh, [LORD,] that You would rend the heavens! That You would come down!"

Stationed in between each person were enormous angels. The angels would respond to each prayer with a cry more intense and powerful than the cry of any person in the prayer line. With the Word of God already open in their hands, the angels responded with Joel 2:13 to each prayer. They cried with a voice like the sea, "You rend *your* heart."

Each intercessor in the line would open his or her Bible and pray. The angel behind the intercessor would respond immediately, and then another intercessor would follow.

"God, rend the heavens."

"You rend *your* heart."

"God, rend the heavens."

"You rend *your* heart."

I watched this back-and-forth interaction for a while. The compassionate, steady gaze of the Father was upon us, the One who was training us and who wanted to purify us. His gaze was so kind and tender. His eyes

DO IT THIS WAY: DAY BY DAY, STEP BY STEP, CHOICE BY CHOICE, AND YES BY YES.

danced with pure enjoyment as the intercessors prayed. He breathed in the prayers, taking in the fragrance that arose to Him.

He said, "I am sending signs to let you know I am coming to help you. The snow is coming as a reminder of righteousness. The rain is coming as My promise to move the heavenly hosts on your behalf, because I want a pure and shining Bride. If you will do your part, I am going to come along behind you and shove you into victory. When you see the snow, think of

Me. When you see the rain, think of Me."

I asked the Lord, "How do I do this? How do I live holy?"

He answered, "You do not have to climb the mountain of holiness and perfection in one day. Do it this way: day by day, step by step, choice by choice, and yes by yes. It is one day at a time, one step at a time, one choice at a time, and one yes at a time. You may not be perfect for the rest of the week, but your next choice can be a yes for Me, and your next choice after that. If you mess up, press delete and quickly get right back into step.

"If you will do the little thing of taking the step-by-step journey, then I will do the big thing and set you free. That which tripped you up yesterday is what you will tread upon tomorrow."

As we ran the race, the wind of God's grace would come behind each person and shove us through the finish line. Each person individually broke the ribbon at the end of the race. All the sin written on each jersey fell off, and the jerseys transformed into pristine white.

*After weeks of unusually warm weather, the April snow came on Friday, April 13th. It began at 8 PM and continued until 6 AM on April 14th. The unprecedented rains started around 11 PM on May 5th and continued for over two days. The nearby Blue River spilled over its banks on the last day of the rain.[1]*

---

*God's passion* and *love*
for us are {deeper} than
the deepest ocean, and His
gifts are {innumerable}.
We could spend our
**ENTIRE LIFE** trying to
search out and understand
the {joy and affection}
that *Jesus Christ* has for
us, and still we would only
**TOUCH** the **MERE EDGES**
of *His great passion.*

# 9. Banquet Table

THE OVERALL SHOUT OF JOY IN THIS DREAM COMES
FROM SONG OF SOLOMON 5:1, WHEN THE LORD SAYS
TO BELIEVERS, "EAT, O FRIENDS! DRINK, YES, DRINK
DEEPLY, O BELOVED ONES!" GOD'S PASSION AND LOVE
FOR US ARE DEEPER THAN THE DEEPEST OCEAN, AND
HIS GIFTS ARE INNUMERABLE. WE COULD SPEND OUR
ENTIRE LIFE TRYING TO SEARCH OUT AND UNDERSTAND
THE JOY AND AFFECTION THAT JESUS CHRIST HAS FOR
US, AND STILL WE WOULD ONLY TOUCH THE MERE EDGES
OF HIS GREAT PASSION. THE LIMITLESS FEAST HE OF-
FERS US IS HIMSELF: EVERYONE IS INVITED TO PARTAKE
OF THE KNOWLEDGE OF GOD AND THE LOVE HE HAS
FOR US, EXPRESSED THROUGH HIS WORD AND SPIRIT.
I LOVE THIS DREAM BECAUSE IT SHOWED ME THAT EVEN
AS HE GUIDES OUR LIVES AND DISCIPLINES US, HE HAS
GREAT JOY IN HELPING US BECOME ALL THAT HE CREATED
US TO BE.

*I* had a dream. I was invited to a banquet given by the
Lord. All of the Church was invited to this banquet.
It was outside in the middle of a wide, green pasture

under a vivid blue sky. The tables were arranged in rows and each had red-and-white checkered tablecloths covering the tables. The Lord had placed large brown baskets filled with the most colorful fruit on the tables for us to eat. You could look at the colors of the fruit and almost taste it in your mouth. The fruit was so colorful, beautiful and inviting; just the sight of it drew your heart to the Lord and made your mouth water and tingle. The fruit represented the knowledge of God and intimacy with Him—knowing His heart, His emotions, and His great love for us. He wanted us to eat this fruit and to feed on Him. I understood that I was looking at a picture of Song of Solomon 2:3-4: "I sat down in his shade with great delight and his fruit was sweet to my taste. He brought me to the banqueting house, and his banner over me was love."

**HIS LAUGH AND HIS JOY WERE UNRESTRAINED. I HAD NEVER IMAGINED HOW MUCH JOY JESUS CHRIST HAS.**

Jesus was so happy that we were eating the fruit. He would walk from table to table, enjoying watching people eat. The more everyone ate, the more He would laugh and say, "The fruit is for everyone. Eat, my friends!" His laugh and His joy were unrestrained. I had never imagined how much joy Jesus Christ has. Psalm 45:7 says He is the most joyful Man to have walked this earth; He is anointed with gladness.

Jesus wanted everyone to partake of His feast. They each responded in different ways. All around me I saw different people, each representing a different facet of the Church, feasting on what Jesus was offering. One group was diving in and eating the fruit because they were leaders. They knew they were responsible for feeding themselves because they needed to feed and lead the people.

Then there were the people who were not leaders. Many of them just looked at the fruit and watched the leaders eat, but did not taste of it themselves. The Lord said, "It is for everyone. The fruit is for all of you. Everyone, eat." But they only looked at the food without touching it. Some did not feel worthy enough to eat. They did not believe the invitation was truly for them.

I realized that everyone has a choice of whether they accept the Lord's invitation or just observe others. All those who only watched and would not partake of the feast eventually ended up leaving the banquet. Although they were still saved, they did not experience the joy of deeper intimacy with God or receive all of the riches He wanted to give them. They heard the invitation to pursue more of God, but chose to pursue something else. When I saw this, it provoked me to dive in and eat as much food as possible from the Lord's table. I didn't want to sit and watch other people eat; I wanted to feast on the fruit for myself. In the dream I ate so much that my cheeks hurt.

I saw a woman who represented worship leaders in the Church putting fruit in her backpack. She kept her backpack full of fruit and ate it all day long as she walked around. She was carrying so much fruit that it was falling out. Young girls were picking up and eating the dropped fruit. They were learning from the woman to feast on the Lord, guiding them to look to God for their own fruit.

Two people who represented children's ministry were tossing fruit up in the air for children around them to catch in their mouths. The two ministers were acting out Matthew 12:14: "But Jesus said, 'Let the little children come to Me, and do not forbid them; for of such is the kingdom of heaven.'"

I saw two people who represented the prophetic ministry in the Church. The Lord stood behind them and said, "They always give twice as much fruit away than they eat, because they want everyone to taste of the sweetness of Christ and the sweetness of prophecy. I see all that they do in secret."

One man who represented the gifts of prophecy and tongues was eating and speaking in tongues. The Lord stood behind him and said, "There is a reservoir of prophetic declarations and prophetic words that the Lord is getting ready to spill out from you. You will be like a volcano, exploding with the prophetic word of God from the inside. The Word will be like lava, setting on fire all who hear it and burning the dross away."

I saw a Southern gentleman who represented the healing ministry. The Lord called him "the one who rallies." He was encouraging everyone just like Jesus was doing. He was eating so much, laughing and yelling at everyone, "He is really, really serious, y'all. You must eat. He really wants us to eat." As he talked, food was flying out of his mouth everywhere and hitting people. He just kept eating and saying, "He is really serious. Jesus is really serious. This is for everyone." Another man and woman from the healing ministry were feeding people who were lame, blind or deaf and could not feed themselves. They were taking fruit and putting it into the mouths of the outcasts.

A man who ministered to the lost was backing up a truck to the tables. He got out and said, "Load 'em up." He was taking the fruit to the highways and byways and telling people about the sweetness of the fruit. Another evangelist took a huge basket of fruit and went into a meadow filled with flowers. He ran through the field, laughing with joy and tossing fruit into the air. The flowers, which represented people, opened their mouths and ate the fruit.

I saw a man seated at the table eating and typing, feeding himself and others through the message he was writing.

EAT, O FRIENDS! DRINK, YES, DRINK DEEPLY, O BELOVED ONES!

I saw a woman who represented believers working in the marketplace. When she ate the fruit, her whole countenance became colorful like the fruit. It was as if she *became* color. The marketplace Christians whom she led took the fragrance of this fruit everywhere, even when they did not realize it, and by doing so led people to the Lord.

I saw two men who were like John the apostle, the disciple whom Jesus loved. They were spiritual fathers with tender hearts like the Shepherd (Psalm 23:1). They were eating the fruit and enjoyed watching everyone feast on the banquet. They leaned into Jesus just as John did, then went to the tables of the people who were not eating and lovingly encouraged them to take that first bite.

I saw many other leaders who were spiritual mothers and fathers. The Lord said they were the shepherds of people's hearts, and a new understanding of things to come—an understanding of John 19:25–27 and Revelation 4:1—would be coming to them.

Many youth were eating the fruit and laughing and throwing it at each other. They were saying to each other, "The fruit is my message." They were part of a whole group, who the Lord called "The Young, Dreaded Champions." I saw so many of its leaders throwing fruit to this army of young men and women of valor. One young leader was singing a new anthem, drawing a new generation of young adults—people of different cultures and races—into a deeper understanding of the love of Christ. A young female leader was throwing fruit to the young people. In all boldness and confidence, she was charging them, "Prophesy!" The Lord stood behind her and said, "You are not only beautiful on the outside, you are beautiful on the inside; your beauty is your greatest humility." She was beautiful because of the great amount of humility she had cultivated.

One man who represented believers who had gone through the dark night of the soul—a time of spiritual pain that eventually leads to greater intimacy with God—was eating with great thankfulness. He was glad to taste the Lord's fruit again. He had tears rolling down his face and he kept saying, "You are so good to me, God. You are so good to me."

I saw a woman who led a dance ministry leading the dancers at her table. They would eat and then they would dance the colors of the fruit. It was not just a dance; it was warfare and prophecy.

I saw a whole section of people eating in the dark. They represented those who stand by night in the sanctuary of the Lord, praying and worshiping. They were laughing, they were loud, and they were really a family. The Lord went over to them and said, "Watch this." He snapped His finger and a glowing, brilliant light appeared in their midst. He said, "The people singing through the darkness will see the Great Light."

As I looked around at those who were feasting at the table, I saw that some liked the place of honor. They liked to sit with the leaders and eat at their table. The Lord invited these people who loved the place of honor to go to a table near the back of the feast. He took them by the hand with great joy and excitedly said, "You get to sit here with just Me and the fruit until you love this place." He did not say, "You *have* to sit here in the place of humility," but said, "You *get* to sit here." He invited them into His great plans of delight and joy even amidst discipline.

Other people who were already sitting in places of humility were also going to experience a change in position. The amount of favor the Lord showed them was stunning. He promoted them to places of honor at the feast, because their only agenda was to love God, to know Him and to seek Him out.

Jesus had great affection for those who found delight in being in the back of the room. I saw two worship leaders. One was sitting alone at a table, just eating, and the Lord took his table and shoved it to the front. It happened so fast that he had to hang on with all of his strength to stay at the table. Then the Lord took the table of fruit the man was sitting at and threw it like a Frisbee right through the sky. He was giving the man a highly visible position, sending his songs out to the nations to give them fruit. The other worship leader was hidden. Jesus told her, "You will surprise everyone and bless the nations with your songs."

As I looked around at the different people and watched them enjoy the feast, I understood that the Lord really wants us to delight in His banquet table. No matter who we are, we can know that He loves it when we enjoy His affections and taste of His fruit (Song of Solomon 2:3–4). The fruit is every facet, characteristic and attribute of Jesus Christ as displayed in the Word of God. To feast on each scripture in the Bible is to feast on the Lord. He invites everyone to eat and drink their fill, to taste and see that He is good.

I knew this **KEY** was not general {understanding} or a word of {knowledge}, but *revelation* on the **END TIME** in particular. It is not just for {one person}; it is for *all* who are **WILLING**.

# 10. What Goes Up

I HAD THIS DREAM ON JULY 5, 2004. I SHARED IT WITH
MANY PEOPLE WHO UNDERSTAND THE STOCK MARKET,
BUT EACH ONE TOLD ME IT WOULD NEVER HAPPEN.
"THE STOCK OF PANCAKES WILL NEVER SOAR," THEY
SAID. "IT WILL NEVER SHOOT THROUGH THE ROOF. IF
IT WERE TECHNOLOGY, COMPUTERS OR OIL, THE STOCK
WOULD HAVE POTENTIAL TO SOAR, BUT NEVER PAN-
CAKES; PANCAKES DON'T HAVE THAT KIND OF POTEN-
TIAL." I REFUSED TO BE DETERRED. I KEPT ASKING FOR
AN OPEN HEAVEN.

On July 17, 2007, the front page of USA Today read, "Stock of International House of Pancakes Soars." The International House of Pancakes bought out Applebee's International, and the stock of pancakes rose dramatically (9 percent gain), just like the dream I had three years prior. (See end notes for more information.)

I had a dream. I was sitting at the International House of Prayer–Kansas City when I saw a white, glowing angel approach me and whisper in my ear, "When the stock of the International House of Pancakes shoots through the roof, be watchful; look up." I knew the stock of IHOP pancakes would be a sign that help was coming (Psalm 121:1-2). The angel continued, "As the prayers of the saints ascend, what goes up must come down. As the prayers of the saints ascend, what goes up must come down." The angel repeated this over and over.

*Wham!* Out of nowhere, a five-by-five-foot boulder fell through the roof right onto the platform. Everyone in the prayer room looked at the massive rock and the enormous hole it had made in the ceiling. In fact, there was no ceiling anymore. We sat in stunned silence, looking up at the sky.

I remember pinching myself, saying, "I can feel my skin, so I must be awake." But the angel ignored my rambling and kept whispering, "As the prayers of the saints ascend, what goes up must come down. As the prayers of the saints ascend, what goes up must come down."

Another angel with great authority took me see a man who was praying and studying his Bible, focusing on Daniel, Zechariah and Revelation. This man represented all who are willing to pursue revelation of the End Times, those who are fully devoted to waiting on the Lord.

> AS THE PRAYERS OF THE SAINTS ASCEND, WHAT GOES UP MUST COME DOWN.

The angel said, "They have been asking for understanding to a mystery in Revelation. After a season, those devoted to God will be presented with a golden key of needed truth." I saw a long golden key made for opening lockboxes. I knew this key was not general understanding or a word of knowledge, but revelation on the End Times in particular. It is not just for one person; it is for all who are willing. I knew the Lord desired that His people would have deep understanding of the End Times, and that Daniel 12:4 and 9 should be relayed to them unto that end—for it is time to seek more understanding of the End Times.

## ENDNOTES

1) Indicating rousing approval of the offer, IHOP's shares jumped 9.0%. http://www.forbes.com/markets/2007/07/16/ihop-applebees-dining-markets-equity-cx_er_0716markets09.html

2) See the official acquisition website for more information. http://www.ihopapplebeesacquisition.com/

3) IHOP Corp. shares jumped 8.9 percent Monday, while volume jumped to eight times its usual level. The Glendale, Calif., pancake restaurant operator said it would pay about $1.9 billion for casual bar-and-grill restaurant operator Applebee's International Inc. *Usually, shares of an acquiring company fall on news of a big purchase*, but analysts said IHOP got a good price. *Shares . . . hit an all-time high* of $64.89 Friday before edging back to end mostly flat. Volume fell Tuesday and returned to more normal levels later in the week. Shares closed $64.46 Friday, up 14.6 percent since the Monday news. http://biz.yahoo.com/ap/070720/hot_stocks_of_the_week.html?.v=1

4) Applebee's shares rose 53 cents, or 2.2 percent, to $24.91 in trading Monday. *In an unusual move for the shares of a buyer, IHOP stock gained even more*, rising $4.99, or 8.9 percent, to $61.24 after briefly reaching a new 52-week high of $63.39. http://www.usatoday.com/money/economy/2007-07-16-4078831354_x.htm

The **PRAYERS** of

individuals,

small groups and

houses of prayer are

**HIGHLY ESTEEMED**

by *God*.

As citizens begin

{to pray} and

houses of prayer {arise},

the *Lord's will* for

the land and its leaders

**WILL BE DONE**

in that nation.

# 11. Kings and Princes

I BELIEVE WE ARE TO PRAY FOR ENGLAND, ASKING GOD
TO BRING LIGHT TO THE HEARTS OF KINGS AND PRINCES,
AND TO ENCOURAGE HOUSES OF PRAYER, ESPECIALLY THE
SMALL GROUPS OF FAITHFUL PEOPLE MEETING IN HOMES.
THIS WILL BRING ABOUT THE PLAN OF THE LORD FOR
THAT NATION (1 TIMOTHY 2:1–30).

I had a dream. It was like I was watching a movie about future events in England. I saw the Lord begin to stir a great number of women and men across England to pray. Small groups, sometimes only three to ten people, met in homes together to intercede for their land and to ask the Lord to raise up righteous leaders. I saw houses of prayer raised up one by one across the nation. Because of this prayer movement, rays of light started breaking through the dark cloud that had shrouded the nation.

I saw that as the people prayed and as houses of prayer began to arise all over the land, God brought light to the hearts of the kings and princes. The prayers of the saints arise to Heaven and light breaks forth on Earth, for what goes up must come down.

In this dream, the Lord made a declaration: "I have not forgotten you, England. I have not forgotten you. There is a young royal who has made headlines from nation to nation. But I will take his wildness and turn it for good. I will encounter him who is red and ruddy, the second-born of his father. He will walk alongside his brother as a prophetic voice, like Nathan the Prophet walked alongside King David. Yet I will also thrust him forth in his own calling. He will walk in a dual calling as prophet to the King and as a voice to a generation. I have chosen the second-born, just like I chose Jacob the second-born—though you call him Harry, I call him Jacob, and he will lead a great Jacob generation.

I SAW THE LORD BEGIN TO STIR A GREAT NUMBER OF WOMEN AND MEN ACROSS ENGLAND TO PRAY.

"The one who will be king will be shown to have a heart like David. Together, the one like King David and the one like Jacob will lead a cry for righteousness in the land. This wave of righteousness will be as a tidal wave, reaching even Australia—and when England reaches out its hands to Australia, they will accept the invitation."

The Lord saw some of the leaders of the land walk up the steps to a mosque, which was called the House of Allah in my dream, and declare their allegiance to a foreign god. They vowed to embrace all religions for the sake of humanity, pledging their allegiance in return for great favor and fame.

The Lord saw and heard those who were in leadership say, "My leadership is inevitable. Even God Himself could not change my position." At that point, I saw the Lord's hand holding a stamp. He stamped the word *rejected* in big, bold, red letters across the papers of those leaders. God was making it known that He has instead chosen leaders like King David— those who have hearts after God (Acts 13:22).

I saw the Lord begin to shed light on the true motives of the leaders of the land; little by little, their hearts were exposed. I saw that the Lord had already been visiting the Queen of England in dreams.

The Lord said, "A great controversy will arise in England as I bring light to the hearts and motives of the kings and princes. A great cry for righteousness shall arise from the people in the land."

The prayers of individuals, small groups and houses of prayer are highly esteemed by God. As citizens begin to pray and houses of prayer arise, the Lord's will for the land and its leaders will be done in that nation.

If the *Church* will

{go low} in **PRAYER**,

we will emerge {unwavering}

in our *faith*,

we will be {untouched}

by the **ENEMY'S LIES**,

and we will {encounter}

the *Lord* in the midst

of the **HAVOC** felt

across the nation.

# 12. Out of America's East

SATAN INTENDS TO INCREASE THE SPIRIT OF WITCHCRAFT ACROSS AMERICA, STARTING MANY FIRES, STIRRING UP SMOKE AND SPREADING FEAR. THIS SPIRIT OF WITCH-CRAFT, WHICH WILL BE RELEASED LIKE NOTHING OUR NATION HAS YET SEEN, IS GOING TO BE LIES FROM HELL: PERSUASIVE AND DECEPTIVE. THE ENEMY WILL LURE MANY TO BOW TO HIM OUT OF FEAR INSTEAD OF BOWING TO GOD IN FAITH WITH PRAYER AND INTIMACY. BUT THERE IS ONE WAY TO FIGHT IT AND TO ENCOUNTER THE LORD IN THE MIDST OF THE SHAKING: GO LOW—PRAY. THIS IS THE PLACE WHERE WE MUST LIVE.

*I* had a dream. I saw a strong spirit of witchcraft come from America's east. It was released through key people in governmental places, including wom-en. Everything coming from the mouth of this spirit is not truth and not the word of the Lord. His heart and His plans are not to be found in the message.

The enemy wants to lure the Church out of its place of power, which is on its knees. The Church must go low in faith and intimacy with God.

In my dream, I had to push my head down to the ground and tell myself, "Go low. Pray." From this I knew the coming battle—the struggle to go low, to pray and to embrace humility—would be hard, very hard.

Lies stir up fear in the heart. Many Christian leaders will try to fight this battle with words, but they will only add to the fear, confusion and havoc being released.

The Lord is inviting us to go low with Him. Going low is the place of encountering God, so it is the place of power and change. If the Church will go low in prayer, we will emerge unwavering in our faith, we will be untouched by the enemy's lies, and we will encounter the Lord in the midst of the havoc felt across the nation.

THE PRAYER MOVEMENT WILL START SMALL, BUT IT WILL END UP AS AN ARMY OF VOICES WHO ARE ESTABLISHED IN THE PLACE OF INTIMACY.

The Church is not just those who sit in sanctuaries on Sunday mornings, but those who pray, those who go low when the land is in crisis. This is His description of the Church from 2 Chronicles 7:13–18:

> WHEN I SHUT UP HEAVEN AND THERE IS NO RAIN, OR COMMAND THE LOCUSTS TO DEVOUR THE LAND, OR SEND PESTILENCE AMONG MY PEOPLE, IF MY PEOPLE WHO ARE CALLED BY MY NAME WILL HUMBLE THEMSELVES, AND PRAY AND SEEK MY FACE, AND TURN FROM THEIR WICKED WAYS, THEN I WILL HEAR FROM HEAVEN, AND WILL FORGIVE THEIR SIN AND HEAL THEIR LAND. NOW MY EYES WILL BE OPEN AND MY EARS ATTENTIVE TO PRAYER MADE IN THIS PLACE. FOR NOW I HAVE CHOSEN AND SANCTIFIED THIS HOUSE, THAT MY NAME MAY BE THERE FOREVER; AND MY EYES AND MY HEART

WILL BE THERE PERPETUALLY. AS FOR YOU, IF YOU WALK
BEFORE ME AS YOUR FATHER DAVID WALKED, AND DO
ACCORDING TO ALL THAT I HAVE COMMANDED YOU, AND
IF YOU KEEP MY STATUTES AND MY JUDGMENTS, THEN
I WILL ESTABLISH THE THRONE OF YOUR KINGDOM, AS I
COVENANTED WITH DAVID YOUR FATHER, SAYING, "YOU
SHALL NOT FAIL TO HAVE A MAN AS RULER IN ISRAEL."

God has raised up many houses of prayer and many ex-
pressions of the prayer movement around the world for such
a time as this. Yes, the prayer movement will start small, but
it will end up as an army of voices who are established in the
place of intimacy—those who are on their knees with a thriving
faith, crying out to the God who answers prayer.

*The Lord said,*
"New York, you have been
{a prisoner} to
your own darkness,
but *I call you*
**THE CITY OF THE GREAT LIGHTS.**
*I call you*
a city that is {set on a hill}
and the **SALT OF THE EARTH.**"

# 13. New York

When we look at New York City, we often do not look past the financial power of Wall Street, the glitter of Broadway and the height of worldly markets and industries. We do not see how the people are trapped in the city's spiritual darkness. But God looks at New York and calls its people out into a greater destiny of prayer and of knowing Him: "The people who walked in darkness have seen a great light; those who dwelt in the land of the shadow of death, upon them a light has shined" (Isaiah 9:2).

I had a dream. I was looking down on New York City from above. It was night, but I could see the lights of the city shining through the darkness.

The Lord said, "New York, you have been a prisoner to your own darkness, but I call you The City of the Great Lights. I call you a city that is set on a hill and the salt of the earth. Therefore, to you who fear My name, on the very corner where the door of devastation was opened, the sun of righteousness shall arise with healing in His wings" (Malachi 4:2).

> "I WILL SPREAD MY WINGS FAR AND WIDE AND, FROM ONE EDGE OF THE CITY TO THE OTHER, YOU WILL BE COVERED WITH HEALING. AT THE PLACE WHERE DEVASTATION OCCURRED, SALVATION, RIGHTEOUSNESS, HEALING AND REVIVAL WILL SPRING UP. I WILL RAISE UP THE TABERNACLE OF DAVID, WHICH HAS FALLEN DOWN, AND REPAIR ITS DAMAGES; I WILL RAISE UP ITS RUINS, AND REBUILD IT AS IN THE DAYS OF OLD."
> —AMOS 9:11

I could see that the Lord already had a space reserved for His house of prayer to overlook The City of the Great Lights. The Lord is stirring up His watchmen so that day and night prayer will go out and rest as a mist over the city.

I saw the Lord focus on Broadway. He had a plan to impact creativity and the arts. A Broadway musical will spring up in the heart of New York with a name like *Out of Egypt*. The Lord will arise and come to the Jewish community and the people living in an area He called the Northeastern Gate. He will reveal Himself as the God of Israel and His Son Yeshua as Messiah.

The musical run will start with a man named Tony and will end with a statuette named Tony. The angels themselves would make the curtain calls. In my dream, I

> I SAW THE LORD FOCUS ON BROADWAY. HE HAD A PLAN TO IMPACT CREATIVITY AND THE ARTS.

felt that the angels might appear during or at the end of the musical, and the natural eye may be able to see them. At the end of its run, this musical will cross the waters of the great deep and land within the walls of Jerusalem with new music and new sounds. It will once again introduce the people of Israel to the Lord God of Israel and to Yeshua the Messiah; the angels will again appear. When this musical lands in Jerusalem, it will crush the idols of Kabbalah.

As the nations
of the earth begin
to *pray*,
{breakthrough} will
happen in many nations.
The {key} is
**SIMULTANEOUS**

**INTERCESSION**

in many lands,
accompanied by
*humility*.

# 14. Key of Intercession

THIS DREAM IS A CALL TO PRAYER. AS THE NATIONS OF
THE EARTH BEGIN TO PRAY, BREAKTHROUGH WILL HAP-
PEN IN MANY NATIONS. THE KEY IS SIMULTANEOUS INTER-
CESSION IN MANY LANDS, ACCOMPANIED BY HUMILITY.
GOD PROMISES TO HEAR OUR PRAYERS AND HEAL OUR
LAND WHEN WE SEEK HIS FACE AND TURN FROM SIN.

*I* had a dream. The Lord handed a key to intercessors across the nations. The key separated into
three unique pieces, but became perfectly entwined,
sealed and unbreakable when put together. It was
the key of intercession. He gave it to the three nations that,
without intercessors, were the least likely to come together in
unity: America, England and Korea.

Written on the back of the key was 2 Chronicles 7:14.

IF MY PEOPLE WHO ARE CALLED BY MY NAME WILL
HUMBLE THEMSELVES, AND PRAY AND SEEK MY FACE,
AND TURN FROM THEIR WICKED WAYS, THEN I WILL HEAR
FROM HEAVEN, AND WILL FORGIVE THEIR SIN AND HEAL
THEIR LAND.

The Spirit of the Lord spoke three words to me and then paused to brand them on my heart: "If My people." He wanted me to understand that it was a conditional invitation.

In this dream, I was taken back into two prior dreams I had experienced and then shown the third part, as if to see how they interacted with one another. First, the Lord brought me back to a dream that dealt with America. He had said in that dream,

"If My people who have been given the key will pray for that which I am doing, a visitation will come to the highest office of the USA. I will turn the president's heart straight into My purposes like a river (Proverbs 21:1). I am going to do what man said could not be done. I am going to supersede that which man says is law. Watch and pray."

The Lord said, "If My people who have been given the key will pray for that which I am doing, then I will also visit England." He took me back to the dream of England's kings and princes, in which He had said,

"I have not forgotten you, England. I have not forgotten you. There is a young royal who has made headlines from nation to nation. But I will take his wildness and turn it for good. I will encounter him who is red and ruddy, the second-born of his father. He will walk alongside his brother as a prophetic voice, like Nathan the Prophet walked alongside King David. Yet I will also thrust him forth in his own calling. He will walk in a dual calling as prophet to the King and as a voice to a generation. I have chosen the second-born, just like I chose Jacob the second-born—though you call him Harry, I call him Jacob, and he will lead a great Jacob generation."

The Spirit of the Lord said, "I will encounter the second-born first and He shall lead a cry for righteousness in England.

My eyes are on one like Jacob and on one like King David. Together they will intercede for righteousness in the land. Though a cloud arises over the land, a great light shall blaze out of it."

The scene changed; I was shown the continuation of the first and second dreams. I saw great fear arising in Korea: murmurings and whispers of those planning evil, darkness and great destruction. The Lord said, "If My people who have been given the key will pray for that which I am doing, then I will also visit Korea."

In my dream I saw that, even as talk of a nuclear bomb spreads throughout the nations like wildfire, something greater than a nuclear bomb will explode out of Korea: the Son of righteousness will arise with healing in His wings. As the Lord's people humble themselves and pray, Korea will be refined in the fire and washed white as snow (Malachi 3:2-3). God will break down the wall between generations; He will turn the hearts of the fathers toward the children and the hearts of the children to the fathers.

IF MY PEOPLE WHO ARE CALLED BY MY NAME WILL HUMBLE THEM-SELVES, AND PRAY AND SEEK MY FACE . . .

As generational reconciliation happens, an unstoppable wave of intercession will spring up from within Korea like a tsunami and will touch many nations, reaching even to the borders of Israel. Yet this wave will not tear down. It will build up and heal. As Koreans pray, they will be made ready for a great move of the Spirit.

Then, with great weight, the Spirit of the Lord said, "Watch for the signs. He who has ears to hear, let him hear. Watch for a brand-new bloom in the desert. Watch for a brand-new color in the sky. Watch for a tsunami of intercession to spring up from within Korea, for this great wave will touch the ends of the earth, even into Israel—if My people will pray."

The sons of Issachar

**KNEW**

{the signs}

of the times and

**WHAT TO DO**.

Whenever we see

{signs},

we need to ask *God*

what *He* is saying

so that we can

**INTERPRET** them

correctly and not become

**CAUGHT UP** with

{the signs}

themselves.

# 15. A Storm Is Coming

THE SONS OF ISSACHAR KNEW THE SIGNS OF THE TIMES AND WHAT TO DO (1 CHRONICLES 12:32). WHENEVER WE SEE SIGNS, WE NEED TO ASK GOD WHAT HE IS SAYING SO THAT WE CAN INTERPRET THEM CORRECTLY AND NOT BECOME CAUGHT UP WITH THE SIGNS THEMSELVES.

*I* had a dream. I was at a gathering that felt like a big family celebration. My children were there, and others had brought their children as well. Most of the people attending served in positions of leadership: worship leaders and team members, small-group leaders, teachers, and the like.

All of a sudden, a gentle breeze began to blow and get increasingly stronger. There was a huge five-by-five-foot picture window that rattled as the wind intensified. The rattling got my attention and, as I looked around the room, I noticed that others were also beginning to pay attention.

I looked out through the window and saw that new colors had overtaken the sky. Instead of white clouds, I saw large crimson clouds and bright green clouds. They were tumbling and billowing and burning bright. It was startling.

> THEN I LOOKED, AND BEHOLD, A WHIRLWIND WAS COMING OUT OF THE NORTH, A GREAT CLOUD WITH RAGING FIRE ENGULFING ITSELF; AND BRIGHTNESS WAS ALL AROUND IT AND RADIATING OUT OF ITS MIDST LIKE THE COLOR OF AMBER, OUT OF THE MIDST OF THE FIRE.
> —EZEKIEL 1:4

We were awestruck by the breathtaking beauty of the contrasting colors. We stood in silence, marveling at the clouds and wondering what this sight could mean. After a few moments, each person began quoting various scriptures as they strained to give meaning to the sign.

"The heavens declare the glory of God . . . The Son is the radiance of God's glory . . . The grace of God that brings salvation has appeared to all men . . . The righteousness of God extends to the clouds . . . Do not put out the Spirit's fire . . . Jesus Christ will be glorified in His holy people and marveled at by all those who have believed."

Though each scripture was a true statement, God was saying something different. They were so caught up in the sign itself that they missed its true meaning: a storm was coming. Fearful dread—the raw fear of the Lord—suddenly gripped me because I knew none of them had interpreted the sign correctly.

THERE IS A STORM COMING, BELOVED. THERE IS A STORM COMING.

Next to me stood a man who was like a son of Issachar. He was seasoned in leadership and had great prophetic understanding because of his many years spent at the Lord's feet. He shook his head as if to say of the verses everyone had listed,

"No, that is not the correct interpretation." In a measured, slow whisper of certainty and sobriety, he explained the sign clearly: "There is a storm coming. Beloved, there is a storm coming."

Signs are meant to direct us into dialogue with God; they are not an end in themselves. We must look past signs, no matter how great or terrifying they seem, and ask the Lord for the right interpretation.

*God* is inviting
the elder generation—
from the {parents} to the
{great-grandparents}—
to *come out* of retirement.
It is **NOT** time to **RETIRE**;
it is time to **RE-FIRE.**

# 16. Turning Hearts

GOD IS INVITING THE ELDER GENERATION—FROM THE
PARENTS TO THE GREAT-GRANDPARENTS—TO COME OUT
OF RETIREMENT. IT IS NOT TIME TO RETIRE; IT IS TIME
TO RE-FIRE. HE HAS PREPARED A PLACE FOR YOU AS A
PILLAR IN A PRAYER AND WORSHIP MOVEMENT THAT WILL
CHANGE THE FACE OF CHRISTIANITY AND WILL LAST UN-
TIL THE RETURN OF JESUS CHRIST. HE IS TURNING THE
HEARTS OF THE FATHERS AND THE CHILDREN TOWARD
EACH OTHER. COME, FOR THE YOUNG GENERATION IS
IN NEED OF YOU.

I had a dream. It was from Malachi 4:5-6:

BEHOLD, I WILL SEND YOU ELIJAH THE PROPHET BEFORE
THE COMING OF THE GREAT AND DREADFUL DAY OF THE
LORD. AND HE WILL TURN THE HEARTS OF THE FATHERS
TO THE CHILDREN, AND THE HEARTS OF THE CHILDREN
TO THEIR FATHERS, LEST I COME AND STRIKE THE EARTH
WITH A CURSE.

I saw a water pitcher made from clear glass. But this pitcher only had only one side, as if someone had cut it from top

to bottom. I knew if anything were poured into the pitcher, it would run right out because the container was incomplete.

I saw it sitting on a table. The pitcher could stand on its own as long as everything was completely still, but it would fall over if any kind of shaking or vibration disturbed it. It was not balanced since it only had one side.

I heard the Lord say, "This glass pitcher represents the hearts of both the younger and older generations. It is incomplete, but I am going to make it completely whole. I am turning the hearts of the children and the fathers toward each other. Both sides of the pitcher must be set in place for the outpouring of My Spirit and to be able to stand in the midst of the shaking."

I saw the following scripture play out in front of my eyes:

> ELISHA HAD [PREVIOUSLY] BECOME SICK WITH THE ILL-
> NESS OF WHICH HE WOULD DIE. THEN JOASH THE KING
> OF ISRAEL CAME DOWN TO HIM, AND WEPT OVER HIS
> FACE, AND SAID, "O MY FATHER, MY FATHER, THE CHAR-
> IOTS OF ISRAEL AND THEIR HORSEMEN!" AND ELISHA
> SAID TO HIM, "TAKE A BOW AND SOME ARROWS." SO
> HE TOOK HIMSELF A BOW AND SOME ARROWS. THEN HE
> SAID TO THE KING OF ISRAEL, "PUT YOUR HAND ON THE
> BOW." SO HE PUT HIS HAND ON IT, AND ELISHA PUT HIS
> HANDS ON THE KING'S HANDS.
> —2 KINGS 13:14–16

I knew Elisha represented the older generation while the king was the younger generation. In my dream, when Elisha put his hands on the king's hands, I saw the king shrug off Elisha. It was as if the younger generation believed they did not need the influence or guidance of the prior generation.

The Lord said, "I am going to change this, because I want

a movement that will last until My return. The dads, moms, grandfathers and grandmothers must be in place as pillars of the movement so it will not burn out."

The older generation represents longevity and faithfulness in the Lord through good times and dark times, through seasons of favor and seasons of demotion. The younger generation represents the youth revival that will sweep through the nations of the earth.

Then the Lord said three things:

"Healing is coming to moms and dads, grandmothers and grandfathers who feel disqualified by their past, for their past is the very reason they are qualified. Come again and find your place on the wall. This generation of youth is in need of you.

"I WILL TURN HEARTS SO THAT LOVE IS THE SEAL UNITING BOTH GENERATIONS."

"Healing is coming to the hearts of children who come from abused backgrounds. Where the older generation has brought them pain, they do not want to open their hearts to them. So I am going to set new spiritual moms and dads in their lives to bring them healing, and their hearts will be softened.

"I will crush the spirit of elitism between the generations, the spirit that puffs up. I will turn hearts so that love is the seal uniting both generations. The youth will run and soar like eagles, and the older generation will stand as pillars in a movement that will last until Jesus Christ returns."

The *Lord* is giving us
a **GREAT INVITATION**
to {lift} our voices,
to {join} the
*Great Intercessor*
and {pray} for
*His friends:*
for the **POOR**,
for the **UNBORN**, and
for the apple of His eye,
**ISRAEL**.

# 17. Time to Dance

THE LORD IS GIVING US A GREAT INVITATION TO LIFT OUR VOICES, TO JOIN THE GREAT INTERCESSOR AND PRAY FOR HIS FRIENDS: FOR THE POOR, FOR THE UNBORN, AND FOR THE APPLE OF HIS EYE, ISRAEL. PRAYER CONNECTS US TO GOD'S HEART; OUR HEARTS ARE UNITED WITH HIS. WE BEGIN TO FEEL THE DEPTHS OF HIS PASSION FOR THOSE WHO SEEMINGLY HAVE NO VOICE. WHEN WE BEGIN TO UNDERSTAND HIS EMOTIONS ABOUT THE INJUSTICE ON THE EARTH, WE WILL ENTER INTO A NEW KIND OF INTERCESSION.

I had a dream. The Lord came to me and said, "I want you to meet My friends." I was excited because I thought I was going to meet Isaiah, Peter or Moses. He took me by the hand and we flew loop-de-loops through the sky like we were in a cartoon. Even though we were extremely high above the ground, I was so aware of not being afraid; I loved just holding His hand and feeling the wind on my face.

Suddenly His countenance changed. He set His face

intently toward Earth and we started heading directly toward the ground in a head-first dive. I thought, *Surely we aren't going to hit the ground*. But when I looked at His face, I could see fierce determination in His eyes.

> THEREFORE I HAVE SET MY FACE LIKE A FLINT, AND I KNOW THAT I WILL NOT BE ASHAMED.
> —ISAIAH 50:7

I knew He had already decided what He was going to do. He was not going to turn around. I felt horrible dread come over me as we kept descending, even though I was holding His hand.

We didn't crash. We exploded right through the ground like a scene from an action movie. I could see the impact as we blasted through the ground. I could hear the earth exploding around us as we traveled through rock, water, and burning fire. The sound was deafening, like the sound of a rocket being launched. I felt the earth pounding my head and rattling my body, and I could feel my skin burning and tearing. I was in immense pain in my dream, yet the Lord's face never turned to the left or right; His eyes were fixed straight ahead.

> "UNTIL YOUR HEART IS TORN LIKE YOUR FLESH IS NOW, YOU DO NOT KNOW HOW I FEEL ABOUT MY FRIENDS."

Suddenly we burst through the other side of the Earth. I stood there looking at my body for a moment, in shock at what had just happened. My skin was lacerated. My body was weak and aching. I was crying because I was in so much pain. I thought, *Surely He sees how badly I am hurt and how badly my skin is wounded and torn* . . . Jesus was aware of my pain, but He made it known that it was not about me. He said to me, "I want you to meet My friends."

He began walking. As I followed Him, I noticed that we were in a very crowded place. I knew it was India. There were little children everywhere who were suffering. I saw some lying on the ground with flies crawling on their skin. As they passed from their horrible circumstances into the next life, He was there for each one the moment they awakened in eternity. I saw beautiful young girls in cages, with whom He continually stood. The Lord calls these seemingly forgotten ones His friends. Not one of them is forgotten in His eyes.

The sadness of what I was seeing, along with the agonizing pain my body felt, left me in tears. The Lord came over to look me in the eye. I thought He had finally noticed my pain and was coming to comfort me. Instead, He revealed my self-centered response and invited me to feel His heart: "Until your heart is torn like your flesh is now, you do not know how I feel about My friends."

He wanted me to feel the pain of the cuts in my skin so I could understand how His heart is torn. I saw children dying, mothers taking their last breath, young girls being sold, and disease spreading. It was more than I could handle. He said again, "Until your heart is torn like your flesh is now, you do not know how I feel about My friends. You do not know Me."

As I looked at the staggering injustice all around, to my surprise, He came near me to reveal His secret weapon against it. He whispered, "It is time to dance."

He began a rhythmic, tribal stomp. His perfect feet with their scars of passion were bringing justice by stomping out the injustice done to His friends. He said again, "Until your heart is torn in two, you do not know how I feel about My friends. You do not know Me."

Then He grabbed my hand and we blasted through the

center of the earth again. I could feel the horrible pain of my flesh tearing away from my bones and hear the thunderous sound as we pushed through layers of earth. When we came out on the other side, we were in some kind of clinic that was cold, bleak and unfeeling. My first thought was of myself and how much pain I was in. I felt as if I had no skin on my bones, like it had all been ripped off. Through my pain, I could hear Jesus say to me again, "I want you to meet My friends."

I looked around and saw trashcans filled with babies. I could see heads and hands and tiny feet filling can after can. Some were still twitching and staring blankly. Some had burned skin. Others sat there unmoving; their heads were crushed. I could not move or speak when I saw them—I just stood there trembling in shock. I realized I was standing in an abortion clinic.

The Lord bent down to be close to His discarded friends. He turned to look up into my eyes and said, "Until your heart is torn like your flesh, you do not know how I feel about My friends. These are My friends."

I was standing there as another baby—a whole baby—was tossed by his leg into the trashcan. I could sense the Lord's thoughts as He saw this: "Silent and forgotten ones, you are not forgotten. You are *not* forgotten."

They were silent in that room, but their screams echo throughout the corridors of eternity. Night and day they cry out, and their voice captures the ear of God Almighty.

I saw a man who had a torn heart, one who cried out for with the babies. I knew that Heaven knows this man's name because he knows the Lord's friends. An unexpected proclamation burst from my heart toward this man: "You do not intercede in vain. Your name is known and your prayers are heard; it is not in vain."

Again the Lord looked into my eyes and said, "Until your heart is torn like your flesh is now, you do not know how I feel about My friends. You do not know Me."

I felt wounded and exposed—wounded in my body and exposed in my heart. As I stood there sobbing, He got right in my face and said in a low whisper, "It's time to dance." With those perfect feet that tread the high places of the earth, He began dancing and stomping right in the middle of the abortion clinic. It was so powerful.

THE JUDGE WAS STOMPING OUT INJUSTICE WITH HIS VERY OWN FEET.

Each time when I was the most broken and the most undone, He would always say, "It's time to dance; it's time to war. To dance is to war." Then He would stomp with a new rhythm. It was not a feeble two-step or purposeless shuffling. The Judge was stomping out injustice with His very own feet. The dance was so full of intensity and authority that it seemed He took up all the air in the room.

He said, "Few have joined Me, but just wait until the earth joins Me in this dance. I am extending the invitation, but you can only dance when your heart is the most torn and broken."

Once again Jesus said, "I want you to meet some of My friends." We went straight through the earth yet again. I could barely stand after we emerged. My heart was broken and overwhelmed. My skin was torn. My body looked as if a bomb had exploded right next to me.

He led the way down a street, walking with determination. I wanted Him to walk slower because I was in so much pain, but my comfort was not His highest priority. He wanted me to feel the pain because He wanted my heart to know it, embrace it and take it as my own so that I would better understand His heart.

He finally slowed His pace enough for me to walk beside Him. As we walked together, I realized that we were in Israel. At times He tipped His head at people as if to say hello, but He never spoke. He would catch someone's eye and tip His head back to let the sun reveal His face. A small flame of understanding started to burn in the hearts of those at whom He looked, and their eyes would widen as they realized who He was. Jesus was opening the eyes of their heart to see Him as the Messiah. Some He tipped His head to were of great authority—the rabbis of the land and those with credibility within the Jewish community. I could see the Lord opening up their eyes with nothing more than a glance. I knew He was appearing to some of the rabbis in the land, igniting the flame of revelation in their heart.

> FOR WHAT HAD NOT BEEN TOLD THEM THEY SHALL SEE, AND WHAT THEY HAD NOT HEARD THEY SHALL CONSIDER.
> —ISAIAH 52:15B

We invisibly followed these rabbis into private studies and quiet rooms of their house. We watched them fall on their knees and cry out, "This changes everything, absolutely everything." The Lord knelt next to them and breathed on the tiny embers of revelation. Little by little, it started to burn and become like fire shut up in their bones.

Right now, they are hiding the fire of revelation and asking themselves if the encounter really did happen. But I saw that this fire would continue to burn until the appointed day when they can hold it in no longer. From the top of the mountains they will shout, "Yeshua is Messiah!"

> THEN I SAID, "I WILL NOT MAKE MENTION OF HIM, NOR SPEAK ANYMORE IN HIS NAME." BUT HIS WORD WAS IN

MY HEART LIKE A BURNING FIRE SHUT UP IN MY BONES;
I WAS WEARY OF HOLDING IT BACK, AND I COULD NOT.
—JEREMIAH 20:9

I looked over and, for the first time, saw tears running down Jesus' face. I could hear Him sigh, "Oh, Jerusalem . . . Jerusalem."

Like Jacob loved Rachel and like Elkanah loved Hannah, I could feel the passion and love Jesus had for Israel. Yet His passion extended far beyond natural love, so He hurts more than a lover does when their love is not returned. He looked at me again and said, "Until your heart is torn like your skin is now, you do not know how I feel about My friends. You do not know Me."

I wept and the salt of my tears stung the wounds of my flesh, yet I could not stop crying. I crumpled to a heap on the floor, unable to stand under the weight of feeling His heart. He leaned down and whispered, "It is time to dance."

Suddenly we were in front of the Wailing Wall. He started dancing a tribal rhythm against injustice. I could feel the power of this dance. It was heavy and burning.

Jesus said, "A new dance will come out of worship and compassion for the poor of the earth. When your heart is the most broken for the forgotten—for those I call My friends—it is time to dance."

*God* {orchestrates} our whole life, with its many seasons, by continually {pressing} *His Word* into us. We {experience} **GREAT PROMOTION** and **GREAT DEMOTION,** yet they both {come} from *His hand.*

# 18. Kneading Dough

GOD ORCHESTRATES OUR WHOLE LIFE, WITH ITS MANY
SEASONS, BY CONTINUALLY PRESSING HIS WORD INTO
US. WE EXPERIENCE GREAT PROMOTION AND GREAT DE-
MOTION, YET THEY BOTH COME FROM HIS HAND. HE
INVITES TO US TO STAY STEADY AND TO EMBRACE LOVE-
SICKNESS FOR JESUS CHRIST REGARDLESS OF THE SEASON
IN WHICH WE FIND OURSELVES (ECCLESIASTES 3:1).

I had a dream. I saw the Lord take various ministries and knead them individually as if they were bread dough. He turned them inside out and pressed them over and over again. God had a smile in His eyes, since He knew what the outcome of the kneading would be, even though the process might look unpleasant to an outsider. He was maturing each ministry with their own identity and emphasis so they could be served to the nations.

I could see that various ministries were in the kneading process right now—everyone was being kneaded, from the core staff to those who are on the mere edges of the ministry—and that the season of baking in the fire was still to come.

Particular ministries will be served to the nations like bread, but that will only happen after the Lord matures them through the seasons of kneading and baking.

The scene and the appearance of the ministries changed. Now each ministry looked like a puzzle. I saw the Lord take hold of each ministry, one by one, and shake the puzzle box forcefully. "There is a shaking and a shift coming," He said. Then, with a smile on His face and delight in His eyes, He said five things as He continued shaking the boxes.

"I am moving those who have been in the front of the line to the back so they will learn the joy and delight of being at the end of the line.

"I am moving those who have been in the back of the line to the front so they learn to embrace humility and to work on excellence and skill. Those in the back of the line will be just as excellent and skillful as those in the front.

"But there are those at the front who already live by embracing the depths of humility; their position will not be touched.

"There are those who, even at the back of the line, are filled with selfish ambition and pride; their position at the back will not be touched.

"Those who feel they are irreplaceable will be the first ones replaced."

In the Lord's Kingdom, we get to the front by way of the back; we get to the top by way of the bottom. I saw some people who, even though they seemed to be following the Lord well, disqualified themselves from

> IN THE LORD'S KINGDOM, WE GET TO THE FRONT BY WAY OF THE BACK; WE GET TO THE TOP BY WAY OF THE BOTTOM.

the calling or position the Lord had for them because of their lack of humility. And that was their choice. Because He loves them and is jealous for their hearts, God will not allow them to excel until they fully embrace the season they are in. Honor and respect are given only by God; they cannot be asked for or demanded. Only those who submit to the process of maturation and who are humble in all seasons will be exalted by God.

> HUMBLE YOURSELVES IN THE SIGHT OF THE LORD, AND
> HE WILL LIFT YOU UP.
> —JAMES 4:10

Whenever {we} make
a **SECRET CHOICE** to
keep {our life}
hidden *in Him,*
it positions **OUR HEART**
to receive more
from *the Lord*
and to give more
of {ourselves}
to *the Lord.*

# 19. There Is a Sound

Have you ever considered that our Father in Heaven sees every tiny thing we do in secret? He knows every motive and intention we have. Whenever we make a secret choice to keep our life hidden in Him, it positions our heart to receive more from the Lord and to give more of ourselves to the Lord.

Then Elijah said to Ahab, "Go up, eat and drink; for there is the sound of abundance of rain." So Ahab went up to eat and drink. And Elijah went up to the top of Carmel; then he bowed down on the ground, and put his face between his knees, and said to his servant, "Go up now, look toward the sea." So he went up and looked, and said, "There is nothing." And seven times he said, "Go again." Then it came to pass the seventh time, that he said, "There is a cloud, as small as a man's hand, rising out of the sea!" So he said, "Go up, say to Ahab, 'Prepare your chariot, and go down before the rain stops you.'"
—1 Kings 18:41–44

I had a dream. I was in the middle of the ocean running on waves. In the distance, I could see that a small cloud in the sky was set in motion—it was coming toward me. I'd never seen a cloud that looked like this one. It was the most shining, sparkling blue I have ever seen. I began yelling over and over, "There is a cloud in the sky, the size of a man's hand. There is a cloud in the sky, the size of a man's hand."

A worship team was near me, bobbing up and down like a ship at sea. I understood this to mean that the cloud arose out of worship.

Two scriptures were highlighted to me at this point.

> EVEN THE NIGHT SHALL BE LIGHT ABOUT ME.
> —PSALM 139:11

> BUT YOU, WHEN YOU PRAY, GO INTO YOUR ROOM, AND WHEN YOU HAVE SHUT YOUR DOOR, PRAY TO YOUR FATHER WHO IS IN THE SECRET PLACE; AND YOUR FATHER WHO SEES IN SECRET WILL REWARD YOU OPENLY.
> —MATTHEW 6:6

The Lord showed me what would happen when the rain fell. I saw the pursuits to which people were giving themselves in secret, whether good or bad. I knew they would publicly give themselves to these efforts with their full energy when the rain came. The coming rain was a catalyst to propel each person along whatever path they were already on. Some would receive the rain as grace. Others were offended by it and further hardened their hearts, leading to judgment, yet both situations were invitations from the Lord to give our lives to Him.

"GRACE LIKE RAIN IS FALLING. COME, GRACE. GRACE LIKE RAIN IS FALLING."

IT IS IMPORTANT TO GOD THAT WE ARE UTTERLY FAITHFUL IN THE SMALL THINGS WHEN NO ONE IS WATCHING.

Some had already chosen to give themselves to true life. Their secret lives were hidden in Christ. Everything they did was done in secret unto God; even when the rains came, they were all the more focused on staying faithful to the Lord under His gaze. They were unmoved by promotion. Many want to be seen as faithful in their visible affairs without aligning their private life toward faithfulness at the same time, but it is important to God that we are utterly faithful in the small things when no one is watching.

I could see God's eyes watching us and everything we did—yes, everything. He was overcome with joy when He saw our faithfulness in the small things, in the mundaneness of life.

Some had already chosen to give their lives to death. When the rain came, the things they were doing in secret affected who they became in a greater way. The rain did not suddenly change who they were or make them holy; it only encouraged them to publicly become who they already were inside. Their secret life was shown before God and before man.

> YOU HAVE SET OUR INIQUITIES BEFORE YOU, OUR SECRET SINS IN THE LIGHT OF YOUR COUNTENANCE.
> —PSALM 90:8

Then in my dream I started yelling, "Grace like rain is falling. Come, grace. Grace like rain is falling." I understood this to mean that rains come in the Spirit to all of us. Those who give themselves to true life will thrive; those who give themselves to anything less will receive their selfish ambition. God is giving time and grace for us to recommit, ask Him for mercy, and confess our sins to one another so we can be free.

The cloud in the sky may not look any bigger than a man's hand, but there is a season of intense rain coming. Because God has such passion for us to rid ourselves of sin, He is inviting us to greater faithfulness in secret.

The *God* of
**ETERNAL BURNING**
is pleased to
answer the {cry}
of *His people* who,
in all **HUMILITY**
and **CONFIDENCE**,
have set their hearts
to {cry out} to *Him*.

# 20. Justice Rolls

IN THIS DREAM, I SAW THE THRONE ROOM OF HEAVEN
AS DESCRIBED IN REVELATION 4. THROUGH THIS DREAM
I COULD SEE THE IMPORTANCE OF "GOING LOW" BEFORE
THE MAJESTY OF GOD AND THE NECESSITY OF WEAR-
ING HUMILITY AS A GARMENT DAY BY DAY, MINUTE BY
MINUTE, SECOND BY SECOND. THE GOD OF ETERNAL
BURNING IS PLEASED TO ANSWER THE CRY OF HIS PEO-
PLE WHO, IN ALL HUMILITY AND CONFIDENCE, HAVE SET
THEIR HEARTS TO CRY OUT TO HIM. LET US SET OUR
HEARTS ALL THE MORE TO "GO LOW IN ALL HUMILITY."
AS JUSTICE FLOWS LIKE A RIVER FROM THE THRONE OF
GOD, LET US GO LOW SO AS NOT TO BE CONSUMED.

I had a dream. I was standing in Heaven on the glassy sea before God's throne. I could see the throne some distance away; it was above the sea and there was One sitting on it.

All of Heaven was so rhythmic. I could hear the waves of the crystal sea crashing. The sound was so loud and bright that it hurt my ears. The tide that came in made a sound all its own, different than the tide that went out. It was the sound of water and the sound of glass at the same time—as if the water was a glassy tide flowing in and out from around the throne.

I could see a green rainbow around the throne . . . the mercy of God. The color itself was thick, as if it had substance and energy within it. I had never seen that color of green before. His mercy gave my soul such boldness to approach the throne, and yet I also felt the fear of the Lord as I watched wave after wave of mercy pulse outward from this One seated on the throne.

I think I was standing on the sea because I don't remember seeing its edge, but I did know that the tide was flowing in and out underneath me. Everything was moving, never stopping, always in constant motion—up and down, back and forth, round and round—as the tide of the crystal sea flowed in and out.

And deep within me I kept hearing, "Justice rolls like a river. Justice rolls like a river."

> BUT LET JUSTICE ROLL ON LIKE A RIVER, RIGHTEOUSNESS
> LIKE A NEVER-FAILING STREAM!
> —AMOS 5:24 (NIV)

I looked up and saw a stream of living water intertwined with a river of fire flowing from the center of the throne. The water that flowed was wrapped in fire, and the fire itself was flowing. All at once, I realized I was looking at a scene from the book of Daniel.

> A FIERY STREAM ISSUED AND CAME FORTH FROM BEFORE
> HIM. A THOUSAND THOUSANDS MINISTERED TO HIM;
> TEN THOUSAND TIMES TEN THOUSAND STOOD BEFORE
> HIM. THE COURT WAS SEATED, AND THE BOOKS WERE
> OPENED.
> —DANIEL 7:1

Over the sound of the rushing water and fire, I could hear the sound of wings. At a distance, I could see extraordinary creatures—seraphim—with eyes all over their bodies. Each eye was opened wide with awe; the One on the throne transfixed them. They stared at Him continually as if it was the first time they had seen anything so magnificent and beautiful. The creatures kept circling the throne and the sound of their wings made a steady rhythm . . . up and down and up and down, smooth and constant, roaring and fearful, never ceasing. I realized the creatures had been doing this since the beginning of time, yet they still could not get enough of gazing at the One on His throne.

ALL OF HEAVEN WAS SO RHYTHMIC. I COULD HEAR THE WAVES OF THE CRYSTAL SEA CRASHING.

I could hear the sound of crowns rolling on the floor of Heaven as the twenty-four elders cast down their many crowns. They do not lay them down or set them down gently. They cast their crowns in awesome, adoring agony, as if to throw every bit of their being, worth and energy before this One who is so holy. They cast their crowns gladly, for He is worthy of their worship.

I heard a voice that came from the throne. I do not know if it was God or an angel, but it was the loudest sound I have ever heard. I felt like I was right underneath a hundred-foot glass wave that was going to crash down on me at any moment.

I felt like I could not go low enough. I wanted the sea to swallow me up. I was quite a distance away from the throne, but I felt like I was right up close. I tried to dive under the waves or swim far enough away from the throne so I could not be found—anywhere but there—but I was unable to move.

There was nowhere to go or hide, though I kept trying.

And still, I was aware of Heaven's constant movement: the living creatures rhythmically beating their wings . . . the sound of living waters intertwined with the sound of burning fire . . . the ebb and flow of the crashing sea . . . the rumbling vibration of the crowns . . .

All the while, I kept hearing, "Justice rolls like a river. Justice rolls like a river."

I could see a huge book with a huge hand touching its cover, preparing to open it. It was the hand that spanned the stars and marked off the heavens, the One who measures the waters in the hollow of His hand (Isaiah 23:11 and 40:12). I could not read the title of the book. A message was spoken and a huge angel flew from the throne toward me. I thought this angel was going to knock me over, but instead he flew right through me.

I looked down and I could see planet Earth. Many heavenly beings were watching mankind constantly; there was much activity happening between Heaven and Earth. Like shooting stars that streak across the sky, angels were descending toward the earth. I knew these heavenly messengers were being loosed to Earth in a significant way. Something was almost ready to happen—new spiritual seasons were coming to the Body of Christ—although I did not know the details.

THEY CAST THEIR CROWNS IN AWESOME, ADORING AGONY, AS IF TO THROW EVERY BIT OF THEIR BEING, WORTH AND ENERGY BEFORE THIS ONE WHO IS SO HOLY.

I saw the Lord pick up a huge wick and drop it to Earth. The wick had three strands entwined together. He stuck the other end of the wick in the river of fire and living water that flowed out from His throne. The wick began to burn, starting in Heaven and moving slowly toward Earth.

As the people on Earth watched the flame coming slowly toward them, some went low and prostrated themselves before God in humble worship. There were others who saw the approaching flame, but did not go low. Those who remained standing were burned like coal; they were consumed by this fire.

I kept asking, "Why?" And I kept hearing, "Go low. Go low in all humility. Pray. As justice rolls, go low. As justice rolls, go low."

When justice rolls from the throne, the only safe place to be is on our knees with hearts that are not offended. When we are offended, we stand up and stiffen our backs; but lovers bow low.

I was so enveloped by what I was seeing that I had to be shaken out of it. The Lord gave me understanding of why I was seeing these scenes of heavenly activity, bringing to my mind two verses about humility. It was so clear, like the finger of God was writing it on my heart.

> THEN HE SAID TO ME, "DO NOT FEAR, DANIEL, FOR FROM THE FIRST DAY THAT YOU SET YOUR HEART TO UNDERSTAND, AND TO HUMBLE YOURSELF BEFORE YOUR GOD, YOUR WORDS WERE HEARD; AND I HAVE COME BECAUSE OF YOUR WORDS."
> —DANIEL 10:12

> THE HUMBLE HE GUIDES IN JUSTICE, AND THE HUMBLE HE TEACHES HIS WAY.
> —PSALM 25:9

Then the Lord spoke to my heart, saying, "Press in all the more in humility, for My justice is surely beginning. The fire straight from My throne has been lit."

And as I looked at the seraphim and elders surrendering themselves in worship again and again, I kept hearing, "When justice rolls, go low. Go low so as not to be consumed."

The Lord gives grace to the needy, mercy to the humble, opportunity to those who resist, and an invitation to all. He is slow to anger and rich in love. If we bow low in humility, He will meet us there.

*Jesus and the Disciples Going to Emmaus*

# Also by Julie Meyer

Forerunner Music announces the release of *Longing For the Day,* by artist Julie Meyer, a longtime and beloved worship leader and songwriter at the International House of Prayer in Kansas City.

This driving yet intimate collection of songs flows from an encounter Julie had while singing with her team at IHOP.

This production's intensely intimate title track connects the core of a believer's heart with the need to see Jesus face to face … to see Him return to Earth and make things right.

Included also is a bonus track in which Julie shares a dream she had about Heaven and eternity. With its beautiful arrangement, the dream compels you to imagine a glimpse into Heaven as Julie shares this intimate treasure.

***To order this CD and other resources by Julie Meyer
and the International House of Prayer Kansas City,
visit www.IHOP.org or call toll-free 1-800-552-2449.***